WE'RE ALL MARKETERS

WE'RE ALL MARKETERS

20 GO-TO PRINCIPLES TO HELP YOU MARKET LIKE A MARKETER

NICO DE BRUYN

NEW DEGREE PRESS

COPYRIGHT © 2019 NICO DE BRUYN

WE'RE ALL MARKETERS

20 Go-To Principles to Help You Market like a Marketer

ISBN   978-1-64137-236-7   *Paperback*

           978-1-64137-237-4   *Ebook*

To my readers,

You have boundless potential and a unwavering spirit, embrace it.

CONTENTS

INTRODUCTION

——

You are picking up this book for a reason.

Have you heard about the power digital media can have on your business?

Have you been looking at launching your first start-up or passion project and want to learn how to market more cheaply with more effectuality?

Are you looking for a resource that will be a game changer for you?

This book will go over twenty principles to help you achieve these goals. Before we get into the principles that will make you a successful marketer, we first have to understand the "game" we are playing.

The world is built on principles, invisible laws and truths that govern our actions all throughout our lives. Principles are not guesses, abstracts, or theories; rather, they are time-tested by existing long before us and long after us. This permanence of these principles makes learning, understanding, and applying them necessary, not just for you, but for those all around you.

How does this relate to marketing?

Marketing is no different!

DISCOVERY

How did I discover these principles?

I wish I could tell you I had a Eureka moment, when I was sitting under a tree watching a Facebook advertisement and suddenly jumped to my feet yelling, "Eureka!"

Instead, the discovery came after many hours of trying to find the answer to a seamlessly easy question: how can I be a successful marketer?

The seedling of this book was born while I was sitting in my nutrition class, frustrated beyond belief. At this time, I was not a marketer; I was a college student who couldn't for the life of me seem to understand this one medical concept. It wasn't that difficult, but my frustration only grows as I see everyone around me grasping it.

This day wasn't the first time I felt this frustration, but as I progressed from nutrition class to nutrition class, the feeling of not fitting in became more evident. For my whole life, I thought I was meant to be a doctor. Everyone I knew was interested in medicine, so I should be, too, right?

Then it hit me: I like nutrition, but I don't want to pursue it as a career. Though it's interesting, I can't conceive of doing it for the rest of my life. This moment was my wake-up call.

Have you ever been there? Maybe in high school, or possibly in college? Or maybe even right now? Regardless, that's what happened to me, and I bet, to some extent, you've had that moment of realization as well.

Free to explore any possibility, any industry, I set out to try anything I found interesting. I started meeting new people who opened up whole new worlds and possibilities for me, but still I didn't find what I actually wanted to do. As I reflected on these experiences, a subtle pattern started to emerge. In each opportunity, I gravitated toward what I would later learn was the marketing component.

Marketing wasn't even on my radar; I didn't know any marketers, or anything about the industry or how to pursue it as a career, but something in me knew it was right for me. Now you may be thinking, "How does a nutrition major who wanted to be a doctor 'stumble' his way into marketing?"

Trust me, I'll get into that soon.

* * *

You are a marketer.

Regardless if you're an engineer, astrophysicist, or top executive at a Fortune 500 company, you are a marketer. This realization was a complete wake-up call for me: there is a whole world of marketing out there, and I want a piece of it.

Yet like any profession, you need a certain skill set to be successful. This skill set is ever changing because of the fluidity of our digitally connected world. One such skill set we touch on in this book is content, and according to a study conducted by Maryville University, "86% of marketers use content marketing as a regular part of their strategy...however, only 36% assess their content marketing expertise as mature or sophisticated."[1]

* * *

The marketing industry is exciting, filled with countless possibilities. I soon learned that as many as 42 percent of companies have hired a designated content strategist executive.[2] I decided to dig more and discovered now was a perfect time to join the industry. Education has never been as accessible, and demand has never been as high. Just consider that in 2017, we saw, for the first time in history, digital spend surpass total TV advertising spend. In the United States, this amount equated to $72.01 billion spent on TV while $77.37 billion spent on digital marketing. I was sold, but there was a problem.[3]

I didn't know where to get started because there is just so much to learn.

The current marketing industry is going through a change, though. A massive gap has opened up with the Internet reaching maturity, and many have yet to grasp the full extent of the opportunity at hand. Yet when I started to research, I couldn't find a simple resource to give me a good foundation in marketing. Frustrated, I decided to set off to try to find the answers myself and create the resources I wish I had when I got started. I just wanted a book of the principles that would help me build a strong foundation so that I, too, could one day be a marketer.

I set off to do just that: create a book of principles from some of the best marketers in the nation.

The principles are:

Principle 1: The new game

Principle 2: Make it spread

Principle 3: Branded

Principle 4: Authenticity

Principle 5: Riches in niches

Principle 6: Culture Role

Principle 7: Attention

Principle 8: End it

Principle 9: Message it

Principle 10: Be perennial

Principle 11: Tell me a story

Principle 12: Social selling

Principle 13: Lead with value

Principle 14: The three Es of content

Principle 15: Content series

Principle 16: Experiment

Principle 17: Resourcefulness

Principle 18: Customer service

Principle 19: Time

Principle 20: Success leaves clues

I come from outside the marketing industry, and I knew nothing when I started.

In this book, I'm going to show you how anyone—even a nutrition major just out of college—can dramatically and rapidly improve their skills as a marketer.

As you begin, you may hear from people who believe that marketing should be left to the professionals.

Yet research has shown that with the increasing needs brought by the Internet, there will be a need for a whole new generation of marketers will to match the ever-growing demand. In this book, I share my unique approach to the principles that marketers use and how you can adapt them to better market and sell your brand, company, or product in this ultracompetitive ecosystem.

So...you've got this!

CHAPTER 1

THE NEW GAME

———

"Millennials, and the generations that follow are shaping technology. This generation has grown up with computing in the palm of their hands. They are more socially and globally connected through mobile Internet devices than any prior generation. And they don't question; they just learn."

—BRAD D. SMITH

THE NEW GAME

Up until this point, you have probably experimented on social media—made a Twitter, Facebook, Youtube, Instagram, LinkedIn, Medium, Snapchat, Reddit, Pinterest, Tumblr, or TikTok, account, right? Maybe you've followed a few people, posted a few things. Have you had any success?

You are now entering a new world of media, called "new social." New social is a term we use to describe the current state of the Internet, where the boundaries of online and offline are blurred. This new age of digital media is only about ten years old, which is astounding considering it has become so intertwined with our daily lives.

Our adventure starts with Shama Hyder, a digital pioneer who is one of those visionaries who saw the potential of social media before most of the world did. Over the last ten years, Shama has become one of the world's most renowned digital marketers.

She is not new to social media; she was among the first two thousand users to sign up for Twitter, the platform which was the basis of her master's thesis. When she graduated in 2008, Shama knew she wanted to work in social media and digital marketing.

This idea sounded great, until she realized that no big company was hiring anyone in social media.

"Social media marketing was such a new field, and in the midst of the great recession companies were unwilling to invest money in this new way of marketing."[1]

"When I was getting out of school, people said, 'Shama, what's tweeter?' or, 'What's the social media thing?' The landscape looked so different."[2]

Faced with the lack of job prospects and a hunch about social media, she decided it was the right time in her life for her to take risks and do what she is passionate about.

Her company, Zen Media, was born. She decided to create a company that would serve to help corporations specifically. However, due to the continuation of the recession, these big companies were still unwilling to hire her company or even consider taking on more risk of losing money. Small businesses had the opposite perspective. "Because of the recession, small brands and businesses were continually looking for different ways to make their marketing dollars work harder for them."[3]

Some of the success she experienced was came from steering her company to embrace opportunities that social media brings on and always looking for ways to bring more value to the end client.

Even more important, though, was the way she recognized social media for what it is.

TRADITIONAL VS. SOCIAL

You can't win if you don't understand how the game works, and that is why it is critical to learn about the new rules. You can't win a game of poker if you don't know how to read your opponent's bluff or when to fold. The same goes for marketing, and one of the key components is to understand the real meaning of social media.

> One definition for social media is where people connect, communicate and, collaborate that is a definition for traditional social media. But there's a bigger definition that I would really encourage everyone to start thinking about, and that's the idea that people are now the media. Now let that sink in, people are now the media.
>
> Social media isn't so much about platforms that are used. People think about the Snapchats and the Instagrams but those come and go. Rather social is about how we make decisions and how we are influenced now. All of these decisions are very social media driven and this gives way to this idea that people are the media. (*2017 Gwyn David Lecture presented by Shama Hyder*)

To see this idea in action, think about your own habits. What is your criteria when selecting a new restaurant to try? Where do you go to find that information?

For most people, there are two options:

- Grab your phone and ask a friend or friends.

- Use a platform like Yelp to read reviews on the restaurant.

Which sounds is more convenient for you? Which one do you do?

For both sources, you rely on others' opinions, but with social platforms, such as Yelp, you are able to not only find nearby restaurants, but also hundreds of reviews from past customers.

What about our movie preferences?

Before going to watch a new movie, where do you go to find out if it was good or not? Again, you can go ask a friend, but what if it just came out or none of your friends are interested in that particular movie?

That's why we go to websites like Rotten Tomatoes before even entertaining the idea of sitting through that movie.

This influence of the collective opinion is the power of social media: you, the customer, completely change how we all make decisions. We used to talk about social media as something we use, but now it has become the ecosystem we call home.

Knowing the power of social media gives businesses and brands a better chance to focus on creating relationships and increasing engagement with their potential customers. To be relevant, brands have to figure out a way to integrate the physical and digital worlds.

REAL WORLD TALK

One example of this principle I have long thought about is what Disney can do at its amusement parks. We all have the experience of going on a fantastic ride, the one on which your adrenaline is high, your breathing is fast, and your heart feels like pounding out of our chest. Possibly this was on a children's ride, but it was a magical experience nonetheless.

Once you compose yourself and get off the ride, you are faced with a choice. Do you want to buy a snapshot of yourself on that ride? You know, the one of you screaming as you are about to go on that wild turn? The one at the peak of excitement on that ride?

If you look at the overall revenue generated from those parks, those photographs make up a significantly small portion of profits, so why not just have kiosks set up that will send you those images digitally for free? It would be a win-win for both you and the theme park.

You would get a great image to post on your social media pages and have a memory to cherish for years to come.

Disney, or whatever amusement decided to implement this idea, would increase brand exposure because of the broad reach that comes with sharing those experiences digitally. As soon as you share it on your social media, your friends will see it. If your friends interact with it, then others will see it, and so on and so forth, causing the brand to spread.

This publicity will showcase the brand more, and, with this small investment with the kiosks, will enable it to better reach new audiences for a fraction of the price.

Another way to do this is to meet people where they are; start listening to your audience and learn to pay attention to what they are saying, which could be positive or negative.

Hearing audience feedback will inevitably begin to build trust, and, with consistency, those customers will see the signal of your brand above the massive heap of information.

With such a wealth of knowledge, the brands that can provide value and essential information in context will see much more attention than those who don't.

YOU ARE NOW READY

"Communication has become more important than ever before; it is not a soft skill anymore. In a world where algorithms and computers are doing so much of the hard work, communication becomes paramount...someone has to be able to take that, explain it, and make sense of it. Things like creativity and communication, these things that we've considered soft skills for so long, are really going to be the paramount skills in the future."[4]

You will learn to adapt to this new world and start to view digital and social media not as separate from the physical world, but rather an extension of it. Technology will bring us closer together as we become ever more immersed in the social media ecosystem of our culture. Focus on ways for your brand to connect these two worlds, leveraging both to reach new customers and keep those that have already engaged with you.

By this point, I hope you are starting to see the opportunity right in front of you, but in case you don't, I'll let the research speak for itself.

WHAT DOES THE RESEARCH SAY

In 2012, "Forbes conducted research to see how consumers engage with different organizations and businesses such as retail, hospitality, entertainment, and financial business through social media networks. They found that a whopping 81% of respondents admitted that recommendations and posts from family and friends directly impacted their buying decisions, while 78% of people said that social media posts of companies influence their buying decisions." [5]

This study was so impactful because of its breadth: twenty thousand people across the United States and the United Kingdom were surveyed.

According to another study by Collective Bias, a leader in shopper-focused influencer marketing showed more exciting findings.

"The survey fielded to nearly 14,000 adults found that 30 percent of consumers are more likely to purchase a product endorsed by a non-celebrity blogger than a celebrity. Of that number, 70 percent of 18 to 34 year-olds had the highest preference for 'peer' endorsement." [6]

Social media is increasingly driving decision-making and influencing us all. This research shows that as the digital and physical worlds start to mesh more seamlessly, a new way of viewing marketing must be adapted to remain prosperous.

MY STORY OF THE PRINCIPLE:

I never really gave much thought to my purchasing habits. I thought I was a logical consumer that only cared about the price and quality; boy, was I wrong. As I began to uncover my own spending habits, I noticed I was heavily influenced by both my peers and influencers on each social media platform. For instance, consider the reason I decided to buy Seth Godin's book "This Is Marketing": my decision had less to do with the fact I wanted another book about marketing from an expert and more to do with several influencers in my community speaking highly of his work and the lessons in his book.

I might have eventually bought it, but after seeing more and more people talking about it, I was compelled to pull the trigger and purchase the book. I know I am not alone because I see it happening all around me, especially on social platforms.

ACTION CHECKLIST

Breathe. Though this might seem messy, complicated, and confusing, I assure you I am here to help. This book will layout all you need to know, with principles like the above one with experts, valuable case studies, and helpful checklists that will have you saying, "I'm a marketer!" by the last page.

THIS IS YOUR FIRST CHECKLIST:

- Start with a piece of paper and at the top write one thing.

- "Today, I am a new social marketer."

- Next below that statement, create three sections.

- In each of the three sections, write down a product you have recently purchased that is outside of the norm. It can be at any price.

For each item, answer these questions:

- What influenced you to buy it?

- Who else do I know who has bought this?

- How long did it take me to buy it? (Was it a split decision or have you thought about it for a while?)

- Where did you first see or learn about this product?

Ask yourself these questions whenever you purchase items outside of the norm. Through this process, you will learn how your fellow marketers are selling to you. The better you understand how your behavior is impacted, the better you will be able to do that for yourself.

That's right, you have taken your very first step to become a new social marketer, congratulate yourself! Now let's keep going; the journey has just gotten started.

"We are all now connected by the Internet, like neurons in a giant brain."

- STEPHEN HAWKING

CHAPTER 2

MAKE IT SPREAD

———

"There are two ways of spreading light: to be the candle or the mirror that reflects it."

—EDITH WHARTON

COFFEE, COFFEE, COFFEE

The best coffee I ever had was Jamaican Blue Mountain Coffee from Starbucks. This type of coffee is scarce and one of the most expensive coffees per pound in the world. The coffee is much lighter than others and feels creamy and smooth with a hint of sweetness. No need for milk, sweetener, sugar, or anything else because it's so delicious by itself.

How much did Starbucks promote me to say that? Nothing. This advertising was not a sponsored deal, nor did I accept any money to say it. I just love the product.

When you have the right product, a compelling story, and market to the right person, you win. Why? That person will tell a friend, who is more likely to try the product on the recommendation of their trusted friend. If they love it, then they will express their love for the product to another friend, and so on. This appealing to the right audience is the principle of how to make your brand's message and offerings spread.

CASE STUDY: STARBUCKS JAMAICAN BLUE MOUNTAIN COFFEE

Starbucks was able to market Jamaican Blue Mountain Coffee to me effectively because I felt they were marking just to me, Nico.

- I like finer coffee.

- I care about:

    - How it was roasted,

    - Where it came from,

- The coffee brands history,

- Its acidity, and

- Its underlying flavor notes.

Maybe you aren't on that same coffee lover level as me, but there is something else that you love. Perhaps it's a specific type of steak, wine, car, watch, or pair of glasses.

We all love different products, services, or brands, and if the product is fantastic and marketed effectively to us, we will tell our friends without even thinking about it.

How can you do this?

You can accomplish this marketing success by learning to make it spread, and that is why I want to introduce you to Seth Godin. Seth is the author of nineteen international bestsellers that have changed the way people think about marketing and work. He is also an inductee to the Marketing Hall of Fame, a member of the Direct Marketing Hall of Fame and the Guerrilla Marketing Hall of Fame. As one can see, he is a decorated marketer with a proven record of being at the forefront of the changes in marketing and branding.

"IF YOU MARKET TO EVERYONE, YOU MARKET TO NO ONE"

Seth based his career on a few fundamental principles, but the one that stands out the most is the ability to use storytelling that makes your idea spread.

"What we are living in is a century of idea diffusion. That people who can spread ideas, regardless of what those ideas are, win."[1]

How is this different from the new social?

Before the maturity of the Internet, companies relied on what we now know as mass marketing: marketing that would appeal to everyone. "What marketers used to do is market average products for average people. That's what mass marketing is," Seth said.

This style of marketing focused on marketing your products to as many people as possible, and, for a long time, it worked because it catered to the average person. This tactic worked because marketers knew people tuned into these platforms were not going to leave, so the companies that spend the most money would reach the most people and, in turn, generate the most return on investment.

" and Mass media made it really easy to spread ideas in a certain way. I call it the TV industrial complex. The way the TV industrial complex works is you buy some ads, interrupt some people, that gets you distribution. Use the distribution you get to sell more products. You take the profit from that to buy more ads. Then it goes around and around," Seth said.

However, mass marketing has dramatically changed because the Internet gave us choice. We now can choose where we spend our time, and if we feel that we are bombarded on one platform, we simply move to the next. In this massive marketing shift, the rules have changed where attention can't be bought; it has to be earned. Consumers have an abundance of choices and very little time, so it has become straightforward just to ignore most of the noise we consume.

> Consumers don't care about you at all, they just don't care. Part of the reason is they've got way more choices than they used to and way less time. And in a world where we have too many choices and too little time, the obvious thing to do is just ignore stuff.

> I think the strategy we want to use is to not market to these *average* people because they're really good at ignoring you. But market to these people (Innovators and early adopters) because they care.

> These are the people who are obsessed with something. And when you talk to them, they will listen because they like listening because it's about them

and if you're lucky, they'll tell their friends on the rest of the curve and it'll spread. (Seth Godin, *"How to get your ideas to spread"*)

BE REMARKABLE, BECAUSE BEING REMARKABLE GETS TALKED ABOUT

If we shouldn't market to everyone, to whom should you tell your brand's story?

"Find a group that really desperately cares about what it is you have to say. Talk to them and make it easy for them to tell their friends," Seth said.

As mentioned above, the Internet gave people the option to choose how they spend their time, with whom they interact, and to what they give their attention. The first step for you, then, is to find fans who actually care about you and what you have to offer.

The role of marketing and advertising is not to overwhelm your audience, but instead create conversion with the people that want to be talked to. With such an abundance of content every day, customers have gotten quite good at tuning out most advertisements. The more you interrupt their day with ads they do not care about, the more money you are simply wasting because they will only ignore you more.

THE FARMER

Before the Internet, a farmer with the best strawberries would make the best sales. Everyone in the community knew that the farmer's strawberries were the sweetest and most juicy;that was enough to stand out when he was marketing his business to people who loved strawberries.

After the Internet, however, the farmer with good strawberries just isn't interesting enough to capture our attention. Now, that farmer needs to develop his brand story and make it connect with the audience. He also has to differentiate his product because regular strawberries just won't do. Knowing this, the farmer grows his strawberries in the shape of hearts with a purple tint. The second farmer created a product with a story—a story worth sharing and a product that would ultimately lead to the idea of his company spreading. This farmer's story and product were remarkable.

"The thing that's going to decide what gets talked about, what gets done, what gets changed, what gets purchased, what gets built is, 'is it remarkable?'" Seth said.

The word "remarkable" in Seth's definition doesn't just mean "neat", but it also means "worth making a remark about." This word is the essence of idea diffusion.

"People who can spread ideas, regardless of what those ideas are, win." –Seth Godin

What can you do to apply this tactic in the real world? First, you have to decide what people want and give it to them— mass media aimed at marketing average products to average people. This strategy no longer holds true because, as mentioned, there is way too much noise, and if your story isn't remarkable, you stand no chance of being heard.

You have to focus on a niche and create a story that the niche population wants to hear about. You want to market your account to these early adopters to gain their trust and hopefully make them love your product so much they are compelled to share it with their friends.

"It's really simple:you sell to the people who are listening and maybe, just maybe, those people tell their friends," Seth said.

The product or service that you have might be great, but if no one cares about it, it won't spread. Second, create a story targeted to a niche segmentation that gets them excited and engaged. You have to aim to win them over because if they are in love with your offering, you have a high chance of them telling their friends, and your ideas will spread. In today's world, with endless choices of products, consumers will only buy from you for two main reasons: they know you exist and they trust you.

Discovering what makes you or your company remarkable and telling that story enables you to accomplish both of these steps by connecting with your audience to spread your ideas and to slowly, but surely, start to build trust. At the end of the day, all storytelling is creating an action for those who want to hear it.

WHAT DOES THE RESEARCH SAY?

Bernadette Jiwa is a recognized global authority on the role of story in business, innovation, and marketing and the author of six best-selling books on marketing and brand storytelling. One of her passions was demonstrated in a speech she gave at TEDxPerth titled "The Secret to Spreading Ideas." She breaks down what she terms "the fortune cookie principle." [2]

"Every product, every idea, and every innovation has two elements: the cookie and the fortune." She describes the cookie, as the tangible aspect, the commodity that one is trying to sell. With this, one is armed with the features and the bells and whistles. These are the ins and outs of the product, but really, with the abundance of options today, these features are not enough.

Then, there is the fortune: the emotion that makes people feel a certain way; the call to action. The average marketer sells the cookie, the product, service, innovation, or idea but, in reality, we should focus on fortune: the emotion that will ignite the customer to take action. The customer will then spread the story far and wide, north to south, because of the emotion"the opportunity is to influence how people feel, not what they think," according to Jiwa.

MY STORY OF THE PRINCIPLE:

Out of all the principles, this principle was one of the hardest I had to implement. Not because it was harder than the others, but because it can often be intimidating going against the grain. As we learned from Seth, being average isn't an option because we will not be able to stand out from the noise. Even if what you are saying is very good, it still isn't enough.

As Seth says, "If it's very good, it's not going to work because no one is going to notice it."

Your goal is to be different from the average, to do something that someone is going to remark on. I slowly started to experiment with this strategy, but the real breakthrough happened when I launched a content series called "#SundayFunday." I was obsessed with showcasing members of my community and all the remarkable impacts they are having on the world, but that content never did well. It was because I was not conveying it in a way that would help it spread.

I decided to do a complete overhaul and try to reposition the content so that it would be different from the rest of the noise. That is when I decided to do something completely against the grain: I posted a video of myself dancing, along with text about those great community members. This video was an instant success, and soon that little dancing video was viral on LinkedIn. I continued to post these videos each Sunday. Before I knew it, more and more people were highlighting others in their community; though I can't take all the credit for this success, I know that idea planted a seed that spread.

ACTION CHECKLIST

- Today is the day we make you, your business, or movement remarkable.

- Step one: Draw an adoption curve. If you don't know what one looks like, Google "Adoption Curve" and go to images.

- As we have learned, we want to communicate our message not to the middle of the graph, but to the two groups before: the innovators and the early adopters.

- These groups will be the most respective to our messaging and be willing to listen to what we have to say.

- Next, figure out who these people are. They are in all industries and tend to always have the newest widgets and, know the latest trends.

- Write their names in the innovator section.

- Make it a point to study on what platforms they spend their time, with whom they interact, and where they discover new products or services.

After some research, it will start to become clear what messages brands use to communicate with them, and it's your job to mimic these with your added twist.

After you gain some traction, you have to ask yourself:

"Would my customers be devastated if we went away today?"

This question will be a way to gauge your success. If you have connected with your audience in a way that makes them feel as if you understand them, then your brand has become successful. If not, it's time to head back to the drawing board and try again;experiment with new niches, different ways to story tell, and different ways to become a household name.

In the next few chapters, you will learn to define your brand, story, and niche, but remember to identify right now what makes you remarkable.

Being remarkable gets talked about.

"We didn't come to the world just to entertain, we came to play remarkable roles, and our reward is to see you doing more than us."

—MICHAEL BASSEY JOHNSON

CHAPTER 3

BRANDED

—

"Branding adds spirit and a soul to what would otherwise be a robotic, automated, generic price-value proposition. If branding is ultimately about the creation of human meaning, it follows logically that it is the humans who must ultimately provide it."

—DAVID AAKER

"You too are a brand. Whether you know it or not. Whether you like it or not."

—MARC ECKO

"OUR BLADES ARE F--KING GREAT!"

—MICHAEL DUBIN, CEO, AND CO-FOUNDER
OF DOLLAR SHAVE CLUB.

These are the words that would launch a small start-up, that practically no one knew about to one of the dominant players in the men's grooming industry.

Is that the secret of being a successful marketer? To launch campaigns with cuss words and dry comedy? Possibly, but you would get a ton of backlash if you were to do that with brands such as Apple, Microsoft, J.P. Morgan, Bath & Body Works, JCPenny. Why? That is not their brand, but it sure is that of Dollar Shave Club, and that's why it works.

When I started learning about brand and brand building, I thought it would be simple. A brand is just a logo and a name, right? Well, that is a part of it, but that isn't the full story—not even close. As I began to study what makes some brands so successful, I began to understand that they all have something more than just the product, service, or commodity they are selling.

"When you are playing in the commodity space, which is to say that everything, more or less, can do the same function such as the same cup of coffee or the same razor you have to find other ways of standing out. For most people, this means building a brand," Michael Dubin said. [2]

We are more than happy to pay a premium for Starbucks, Whole Foods, and Lululemon. Not because it is necessarily better, but because of the brand, identity, and the story of that company. Each sells a commodity. Starbucks with its coffee beans, Whole Foods with its produce, Lululemon with its leggings, and Dollar Shave Club with its razors.

Why do these companies continue to thrive? Brand.

"THE RAZOR FORTRESS"

Michael Dubin, a marketer at the time, set out to do exactly that: build a brand—a razor brand. In 2011, while at a cocktail party, Michael connected with a friend's father-in-law. During the conversation, Michael learns from the man that he has a warehouse full of razor blades from a past venture that he is trying to liquidate. Fascinated with this news, he and the man continue to chat about their frustrations with buying razors and how they wished there was a more straightforward way to do it.

"The razor buying experience was painful because of a few factors such as the exorbitant prices of razors that would have to be replaced often." [1] Michael was also astounded by the fact that to buy razors, men had to get a special cage, the "razor fortress," opened by an employee. Why couldn't a person have the razors show up at their house for a dollar? At the time, subscription services were on the rise, and he was fascinated with a solution like this.

"I, much like most entrepreneurs, saw an opportunity and had an opportunity to go right after that," Michael said.

Within a week www.dollarshaveclub.com was registered.

SHAVE TIME, SHAVE MONEY

Selling razors was no easy undertaking. At the time, Entrepreneur, estimated that Gillette had 72 percent of the market share before Dollar Shave Club entered the picture in 2012.[2] These were massive numbers, but fortunately for the company, Michael developed a strategy that is still in use today.

Dollar Shave Club follows a very simple brand template, which is to "demonstrate the readiness of the problem, demonstrate the goodness of our solution and do it in a really relatable way."

Michael took a look at what the industry leaders were doing. He had to "find a different way to stand out because there were a lot of players in the space." After a short while, Michael noticed that while other brands like Gillette were interested in showing off the newest bells and whistles of their latest product, the average man was left with more questions than answers.

"Companies tend to make things more complicated trying to justify all the neat features that their widget, products or services have," Michael said.

That is when the answer became as clear as day.

The problem: buying razors had become a horrible, mundane, and often painful experience that men all across America had to deal with continually.

The solution: a full-scale men's club—a subscription-based grooming brand with personality—that men identify with.

The message: Men wanted something simple, a product that did what it said it would do. That product is precisely what Michael set out to create. Michael's market was people who shave, but he had to start small and find a niche. His niche became men ages twenty-five to fifty who shave. He decided he had to make his brand resonate with this market, and while others were going more serious, he decided to make his funny. With a $4,500 budget,

Dollar Shave Club created a video that would speak to their market, both simply and humorously.

On March 6, 2012, "Our Blades Are F--king Great" video was launched and was an instant success. The video shows Michael simply describing the razors as he walks through the warehouse. While he does so, he encounters a baby shaving a man's head, a scene in which he used a machete to cut some tape, and a leaf blower to blow hundreds of dollar bills around.[3]

Within forty-eight hours, over twelve thousand orders were placed, and the video was a viral success. The video was able to advertise without seeming like it. It created air cover for men to share a seamlessly funny video with others just like them. It created the context for face-to-face interactions that, in addition to it being shared all over social media, expanded the brand's reach. Secondly, the video demonstrated men's pain points with razors and a simple way to fix them. The video showed that simple storytelling, with a comedic twist, could stand above the noise and create massive amounts of interest.

"People feel an emotional connection to this brand. And that reflects a larger theme in business today. If you want to be successful you have to create an emotional connection with your customer; you have to have a conversation with your customer. You don't want to talk at your customer," Michael said. [4]

The success didn't just stop there: Dollar Shave Club expanded, creating more media through which to distribute their simple message, including their own online men's lifestyle magazine called *MEL*, a humorous pamphlet called "Bathroom Minutes," and several podcasts. Dollar Shave Club didn't do anything revolutionary; they were selling a brand.

"Part of this is creating a meaningful impact on our members' lives. In each package to our members, there is always insightful and fun content; for example, Dollar Shave Club Bathroom Minutes, alongside their Dollar Shave Club products. Through this 'magazine,' we not only let our members know what we're up to, but we also help members support other members," Michael said.

DOLLAR DOLLAR BILLS Y'ALL

The company took a stand, through their marketing, messaging, and just overall branding; they took the stance of the rebel. This stance is what today's customer craves: an authentic brand, a brand that they can be behind, and a brand that stands for something more than just their product. In a sense, much as Simon Sinek has repeated time and time, "People don't buy what you do. They buy why you do it." Give them a brand that stands for something.

Dollar Shave Club became an established brand: a brand that struck a nerve with the American people and a brand that people could identify with and stand by, and it hasn't stopped growing since. The company was acquired for a reported $1 billion in 2016 by UK-based company Unilever. At the point of purchase, Dollar Shave Club had an estimated 16 percent market share of the razor industry.[5] In only a few short years, the company has risen to be a market leader and shows no indication of slowing down.

It accomplished all of this success by focusing on building brand to a good product.

WHAT DOES THE RESEARCH SAY

"With so many direct and subliminal messages flooding the senses, it's becoming increasingly challenging for brands to gain the attention of their target market. This is where brand differentiation comes in. When you individualize your brand from the competition in a way that's relevant to your customers, you create a relationship, establish credibility, and ultimately increase their loyalty."[6]

How can you stand out from the crowd? What distinguishing trait encompasses your business? To be successful, a differentiator must be:

- True

- Proven

- Relevant

Take Whole Foods, for example.

"Shopping at Whole Foods isn't like shopping at an average grocery store. They combine knowledgeable and approachable branding with healthy lifestyle options, going beyond groceries and leveraging their shopping experience as a whole experience. Offering local and healthy niche brands to a variety of customers with differing health needs helps drive the point home that they value and provide for their customers with a variety of dietary needs." [7]

Key points:

- They turn a regular day-to-day activity into a lifestyle choice.

- They provide a pleasant, hassle-free shopping experience.

- Customers feel like Whole Foods is their go-to healthy food mecca.

MY STORY OF THE PRINCIPLE

I never understood the extent of the influence a brand can have until I started to write this book. I was always under the impression that I was a purely logical consumer, looking for the best deals and highest quality items, until I closely examined my purchasing habits. For example, I was convinced that I bought my Apple Macintosh computer because it was the best on the market. Though it has exceptional qualities, it was nowhere the best on performance, price, or quality. When I made the purchase, I was not just buying a computer; I was buying an APPLE computer. I was buying the brand—not just any brand, but, as we saw in 2018, the world's most valued brand. We make decisions such as the one I did all the time, maybe not with all products, but each of us has a select few brands that mean more to us than the actual product.

This influence is the exact reason why you have to prioritize brand. I have seen this strategy work time and time again. Whether it is for me or the clients I serve, brand enables you to stand out from the crowd. Not because people are always buying just your product or service, but because they are buying you and your brand. Brands enable us to show outwardly what we feel internally. Why else would we wear clothing with brand logos prominently on them? Because it shows the world what we think on the inside. That is why we care about the brand; that's why we don't mind paying a premium on certain items as long as we like that brand. I can't say it enough: brand isn't a nice to have, it is a must-have.

ACTION CHECKLIST

- For this checklist, we will be using the same formula as Michael did with Dollar Shave Club.

- Start by writing down the problem.

  - For Michael, it was that buying razors had become a horrible experience. What is the problem you are trying to fix?

- Next, write down the solution.

  - For him, it was the razors shipped to a person door. What's yours?

- Write down the message.

  - Write down who your target audience is and how big brands market to them. Most big brands will have a traditional way that they market to their audience. Think about all the commercials you have seen for a man shaving; they are all the same.

- Focus on the content they naturally consume.

  - Men that Michael marketed to loved watching and sharing funny videos.

  - Thus, Michael saw an opportunity that his competitors hadn't seen before and built a brand in that niche.

- Put all of these factors together and you have your tentative brand.

- Test what you have created, see if it sticks with your audience, and change as needed.

"Your brand is what other people say about you when you're not in the room."

—JEFF BEZOS

"If you don't give the market the story to talk about, they'll define your brand's story for you."

—DAVID BRIER

CHAPTER 4

AUTHENTICITY

———

"Authenticity requires a certain measure of vulnerability, transparency, and integrity."

—JANET LOUISE STEPHENSON

"The keys to brand success are self-definition, transparency, authenticity, and accountability."

—SIMON MAINWARING

TRUST ISN'T A RIGHT; IT'S EARNED.

How did you build trust with your spouse, your coworkers, or that nice waitress at that restaurant down the street? OK, maybe not the waitress, but for the other two, and for so many different relationships in our lives, trust stems from being our authentic self.

Being authentic can bring us closer, deepen our relationships, and make them stronger, but the principle can also work to push us away.

Think of someone or some company that you actively avoid. Why do you feel that way? Most of the time the reason can be boiled down to a lack of trust in some capacity. With so much competition between companies, brands can no longer rely on being the only choice for their selected items.

 Look at the search amount of options that exist when you Google the word "shampoo." In case you were curious, in June 2019 it generates 337,000,000 results.

What can we do to stand out from the thousands of other brands out there? By being authentic.

EASIER SAID THAN DONE

Authenticity will help your brand create real, lasting relationships and trust with customers, trust that will turn them into raving fans and create an environment that will make them want to tell all their friends about who you are and what you do. To learn how to gain their trust and create this competitive edge, let's turn to professor Krista Fabrick. She is a successful marketer, speaker, and marketing professor who has helped brands of all sizes understand their brand and how to market authentically online.

In mid-2018, Krista helped me craft my message and how to share that message in an authentic way. It was because of this coaching that I asked her to help me teach this principle to you.

Much like me, Krista never knew she would end up in marketing. As an undergraduate in college, Krista focused on international management at Pepperdine University in California. "My coursework focused not just on business but an array of courses such as political science and communication but none to do with marketing."

Straight out of college, she decided to go directly into sales at First American, individually selling to small realtors, real-estate companies and appraisal companies. While at this first job, she became exposed to marketing. Slowly, she discovered a love and talent for marketing.

In a short span of time, a coworker of hers connected her with his wife, who had started a marketing agency and was at the point where a full-time employee was needed. Krista felt herself being pulled ever closer into marketing and decided to take a leap. She accepted the position and became hooked.

"Over the years, I have worked in numerous avenues of the marketing field from a startup boutique agency to a large agency, working hands-on with clients such as Verizon Wireless."

"What I have learned is that there are patterns that arise over and over again. From big to small companies, one constant that is prevalent to all successful ones is how authentic they are."

So that's it: I just have to be authentic? Yes, but before you move to the next chapter, think back to the chapter of brand. It's one thing to say you are trustworthy, but it's a totally different ball game to show someone. That's what you will learn next.

MAKE IT STICK

Krista discovered there were always some constants in successful marketing initiatives, even if media and platforms changed. When "one is trying to be something that you are not, whether it's for your company or personal brand, is never going to last long term."

For example, during her career, Krista had worked for a person that would try to market the clients brand in an inauthentic way. Usually, this took the form of sacrificing company values or relationships to achieve short-term monetary gains. That person didn't realize this choice did produce short-term success for her clients but sacrificed success in the long run. It came to the point that she lost all of her clients and was forced to dissolve her company.

"You have to be true to who you are because one can only keep a facade up for so long before it all comes crumbling down."

We have all seen people, especially in the business arena, bend their values a little bit too much to ensure they remain appealing to a new group of people, only to lose their core supporters in the process.

How do you reduce this risk? It starts before you start marketing.

According to Krista,

> Before brands can even move forward with creating marketing, they have first to figure out who they are. A lot of brands fly by the seat of their pants. This means that they decide a course of action as they go along, using others initiatives and perceptions rather

than metrics and reality. For smaller companies, many of them have not prioritized what they want their brand to mean, what they want their brand to stand for and what their brand's mission, vision, and values are. For a much larger business, it can be that the brand has been distorted and changed as the company has gone through times of growth. They too have to go back to the basics and establish the answers to the above questions.

"SHOW AND TELL"

We know we have to be authentic, but how can we show our authenticity to the world? Well, this question comes at a perfect time in history, where marketing and branding costs have been reduced drastically.

Krista, throughout her career, has seen companies of all sizes and throughout many industries have marketing budget cuts. These cutbacks can come in the form of a reduction in time, budget, or resources, with an unfortunate side effect often involves less business and sales. One benefit that has arisen to help curve the effects of reduced marketing budgets and what we will be focusing on is social media.

"Social media platforms offer low-cost marketing solutions, but the flip side of the coin is that appropriate time allocation has to be assigned to manage the social media accounts," Krista said.

This management comes in the form of creating authentic messaging, content, and engagements with customers on platforms that they are natively using.

"Authenticity can be expressed through numerous avenues either through text, audio, or video sources."

Let's take a video as an example. One advantage of video is that it makes it challenging to hide your true intention because we are innately good at reading people in person. There are time-tested actions that indicate to us when someone is not being truthful because it is hardwired into us. Video is the next best way to understand someone's true intent.

As the video plays, we are able to watch the person's body movements, hear the tone of their voice, and pay attention to all other nonverbal cues. Altogether, we are able to come to a conclusion in very little time, especially with the adoption of features such as live streaming and short story features that promote raw, real-time storytelling.

"Video will look different to each company and industry, but the fact remains that it is one of those tools that have a proven track record because we have a chance to engage much deeper when we can see and hear someone," Krista said.

Video is just one medium. We can do the same for audio and text-based messages. With each piece of content, your goal is to present your story and message in a way that is real to you and craft the opportunity for your audience to build trust with you.

With this trust, relationship begins to form between consumers and brands. These relationships open the door for customers to support the company by purchasing their products and services, which will have a more massive payout at the end.

And the best part?

This relationship-building is done at scale.

"The internet has made us more transparent than ever before." This transparency is a massive advantage for brands like you who have the time and effort to create meaningful relationships at scale. Authentic content for your brand will enable customers to build a relationship on trust and lead to increase loyalty.

For those who have trailed away from who they are, the influence of authenticity can be a liability. Fear not: with a bit of work and emphasis on what the brand stands for, and ways to communicate that message, brands will be on their way to creating loyal customers.

WHATS THE RESEARCH SAY?

Brand authenticity is now grounded in the overlap between what a brand does and what consumers expect from that brand. How do we define authenticity? The best definition is from *The Journal of Consumer Psychology* which describes it as "the extent to which consumers perceive a brand to be faithful toward itself, true to its consumers, motivated by caring and responsibility, and able to support consumers in being true to themselves."[1]

Why does authenticity matter?

In 2013 the Boston Consulting Group surveyed 2,500 American consumers and found that being authentic was indeed one of the main qualities they said would attract them to a brand. For younger "millennial" consumers (born between 1980 and 2000), it was second in importance only to rewarding their loyalty with discounts.[2]

Authenticity has thus become a staple and has elevated companies by not only to brand storytelling but in every part of the customer experience—from weekly newsletter to email and everything in between. To be authentic means to uphold a certain level of integrity which includes total honesty and transparency. And this makes sense; if we see that authenticity is what works, it can serve as a competitive advantage and a way to cut through all the noise.

As it turns out, most consumers aren't looking for picture perfect ads or overly produced digital experiences. They want the authentic and trusted content that their friends, family, and peers are sharing on social media everyday—organic inspiration and validation.[3]

So give the people what they want and crave.

MY STORY OF THE PRINCIPLE:

This principle has been one of my favorites both to learn and teach, just because it is so practical. There will never be someone exactly like you, with the same experiences, thoughts, ambitions, and desires. Thus, it is imperative that you be true to who you are and live a life being your authentic self. As you have noticed through a few of the chapters, there is so much content and information out there that it can almost seem too intimidating to start. I felt like that; I always questioned, "Why would someone listen to me? Will this help someone? Will anyone listen?" Well, what I have subsequently learned is all these questions would be answered once I committed to being authentic, to show up without a shadow of a doubt and be who I truly am.

From this, the right type of people will gravitate toward you and your messages. The last part of this principle is to experiment. When I was going through what I deam my quarter-life crisis, I learned I didn't know the real authentic me. If this is you and your brand, well, then, you have to experiment. Put messages out there and create content; from this experimentation, you will learn what resonates with you. People want the real you, the true and authentic you.

Give the people the authenticity they deserve.

ACTION CHECKLIST

- Identify the subject of this exercise:

  - Your personal brand

  - Professional brand

  - Business brand

- Write down up to five values and believes that brand stand for today.

- If you are happy with it, move forward; if not, use this moment to redefine it.

- Next, ask fifteen people what brands do to showcase those values and beliefs:

  - Five clients or employees

  - Five friends

  - Five acquaintances

- Next, look at it objectively: do your current actions both with online and offline marketing match with what the people said?

  - Does each interaction with a potential client or customer make them feel that way?

  - Are your marketing efforts authentic to that message?

- Now, you have the feedback to create some sample content, whether it is through video, audio, or text. Take your time to write out some tweets for Twitter, create some videos for Facebook, or record a simple voice message of you talking about your brand.

- Share these pieces of content with your most loyal customers and brand enthusiasts and pay attention to their feedback. Test and continue to tweak your plan and content until you have a personalized, authentic brand message and content that supports it.

- Now, go out and create marketing, content, and messages that revolve around your statement.

"Mass advertising can help build brands, but authenticity is what makes them last. If people believe they share values with a company, they will stay loyal to the brand."

—HOWARD SCHULTZ

CHAPTER 5

RICHES IN NICHES

"If everybody is doing it one way, there's a good chance you can find your niche by going exactly in the opposite direction."

—SAM WALTON

"Very narrow areas of expertise can be very productive. Develop your own profile. Develop your own niche."

—LEIGH STEINBERG

LAMBORGHINI VS TOYOTA

You are in the market for a new car, but where do you start? Well, it depends on what you need, right? A family of six probably will not go to a Lamborghini dealership, nor should they. Lamborghini doesn't cater to this family's car need; for a family of six, you would go to Toyota or Ford. Let's say one of the children grows up, and at twenty-something works on Wall Street making high six figures and wants a fast sports car—Lamborghini is the perfect niche car.

It would be a waste for Lamborghini to market to that family of six; they have different needs and desires. The company can come out with an SUV—they have the capital and manufacturing expertise to do so—but they don't. Why? Because of its off-brand. It's not their niche.

Lamborghini has a niche to which it markets and sells its cars. So does Tesla, Ford, Kia, Toyota, and every other car maker.

One of the hardest things for most businesses to understand is that they can't be everything to everyone. Just ask Greg Head. Greg started his career in the technology sector and quickly realized it was going to become a massively integrated part of our existence. His success came from finding his niche. In this chapter, Greg will walk you through how to identify your niche and become laser focused in marketing there.

When Greg entered technology, many companies were creating a wide variety of products. They would ride the trends, creating dozens of different products. While some were following this strategy, others like Greg were just focusing and niching down on specific software solutions. Each one of the companies he proceeded to join, whether as an employee or cofounding, focused on solving a particular problem for a specific group of people.

TRY TO PLEASE EVERYONE AND YOU WILL END UP PLEASING NO NONE

Why is having a niche so important? With so many options today, only the best is good enough. Let's do an experiment. What brand do you think of when you think of a smartphone?

I bet you instantly thought of a specific brand.

"We won't give ten people the best title in the world, only one or two get that title. That's why everything ends up as one or two in the end. When you start, you want [to be] many things to many people. But the outside world is going to demand from you to focus. Are you the best in the world at that specific thing? [for example] when you think of smartphones you think of Samsung and Apple," Greg said.

Both brands stand for something specific, have specific customers, and market explicitly to them because both have a specific niche that enabled their rise to the top of the industry. They didn't try to be everything to everyone; instead, they tried to matter to someone specific. Marketing to a niche isn't just limited to smartphones—take one of the largest companies in the world.

"We can look at Amazon and say gosh they sell everything that you can buy with one click. But wait a minute, how did they start? They started with laser focus; they just sold books online that people would buy through a browser with a credit card. Amazon started off in a niche by selling just books to people online. To most people, this was a crazy idea because at the time only ten percent of people bought books and only ten percent of people would buy products online," Greg said.

They did that until everyone understood what they offered and then they started adding items.

Now we know Amazon as the company from which to buy everything online, but it started by becoming tunnel focused on over-satisfying a handful of people before even considering expansion.

"SHOW ME A COMPANY THAT GREW UP FAST, AND I COULD SHOW YOU A COMPANY THAT IS NARROWLY FOCUSED."

—GREG HEAD QUOTE

In the new game, there is a lot of opportunity, but they aren't in the masses—they are in the niches. Your goal is to find your niche and market there.

Let's take an example of a chef. He is a culinary wizard and can cook any food you ask him to make. He decides to start a restaurant with the theme any and everything. This theme is fine in the beginning, but if he can cook anything, people will just get bored and move on.

Why? Because the chef isn't playing in the edges, he's playing in the middle, and the middle is boring. The same goes for marketing.

What is the magic trick of great marketing?

Most companies, when tasked with the challenge of marketing, tend to focus on emailing more or designing a prettier website. These tactics don't move the needle a lot, and suddenly you are all the way back at square one.

Their strategy most of the time is to become more things to more people. The magic is to do the reverse of this.

The trick is narrowing in on who you are standing for, what you do and why people should believe you.

IF CHICK-FIL-A CAN DO IT, SO CAN YOU

Any restaurant you see can serve any food within twenty-four hours. McDonald's, for example, could make Thai ice cream tomorrow if the world depended on it, but they don't. Chick-fil-A could make a burger in five minutes—they have all the equipment, labor, and space to do so—but they don't. Chick-fil-A has risen to be one of the largest fast food restaurants in the country, and they have no monopoly on the chicken sandwiches, so why don't they serve hamburgers?

Because they are known as being the best at something to someone specific. They know their niche and they stay in it.

"While some critics believe they do not serve the good sandwiches, the public, on the other hand, keeps going back because they are known as the best, and that's the game that is being played."

To be recognized as the best at something, you have to declare a specialization, we do these things, and we are the best at just that. There is no way you can be known as the best unless you do one thing for one person. This is the essence of product market fit; you have the product (what you do) and the fit (who you do it for).

Understanding this is what separates brands and Greg shares in-depth that people will not hear what you are unless you're entirely clear at what you are not. For Chick-fil-A, their mascot is a cow which is an outward expression that they don't sell cheap hamburgers.

According to Greg,

> If you doubt the magic trick take a look at the restaurants with the most extensive lines, practically every time it is a restaurant that serves a specific type of food to a particular clientele.

> You go back to Facebook [early beginnings], it was just at Harvard before it was at other ivy leagues. You go back to Walmart, they spent seven years in Northwest Arkansas in the towns that Sears

and Kmart would not go to before they started moving on.

You have to go through that pinhole to be focused enough so the outside world will recognize you as a leader.

Once you understand this principle, you can see it everywhere. In health care, for instance, we line up for specialists. The general physician is one who has experience in a little bit of the knee, elbow, and spine, yet no one lines up for that. Those people who are essential to someone specific, such as the knee doctor for sports athletes, have the highest demand and get paid more considerably more than their counterparts.

This is counterintuitive to most because we are conditioned that to get more, we need more tactics, more services, or a bigger audience, but more growth actually comes from less.

WHAT DOES THIS MEAN FOR YOUR MARKETING STRATEGY?

A clearer and more precise message will be a stronger message for your audience. It will resonate more with them, but in order to do make it strong, we have to say "no" more often than we say "yes." With digital media, it can be tempting to want to create content for everyone. It's so easy to write one blog about search engine optimization (SEO) and then another about the hottest stock on the market. With so much content produced every day, it is impossible to market when you try and be everything to everyone. The more you are not everything to everyone, the more the world hears you.

"Your job is to find a focus, who is the unique target market that you're selling to. What is it you sell to them? What is the key benefit to the world."

You have ways to say a thousand things every day, a thousand different ways and to a thousand different people, but so does everyone else. Focus on a market and stay there.

CASE STUDY: RIVVLY, INC.

Defining Target Market

"Defining a target market is like holiday shopping; overwhelming at first but it can be done and, if done thoughtfully, the result is magic."

—SASHA ROWE, FOUNDER & CEO, RIVVLY

Rivvly is a knowledge process outsourcing firm, meaning they procure talent and clients needing that talent, connect them, and then manage the relationship. One example of this relationship is virtual assistants. Sasha Rowe had an interesting approach to defining their target market because, as a multifaceted business model, Rivvly actually had two target markets to define. Defining the market for talent came first, mainly because without the talent, there were no clients.

Everyone wants to work from home though, right? How do you pick an industry? How do you find these people? The prospect of opportunity was thrilling but exhaustingly broad.

Rowe didn't want to limit the business, but knew learning how to swim in the ocean wasn't the answer either. Reverse engineering the start small, test, and adjust model taught in most entrepreneurial texts, Rivvly was able to define a niche market that *worked* by starting board and narrowing their target market using key metrics that filled the biggest gaps. Basically, funneling the market until it produced the most ideal talent pool and the most ideal client and then focusing on that.

Marketing Strategy

Being an industry leader in branding, Rowe kept all of Rivvly's marketing in-house. "The marketing strategy started a lot more basic than I expected, or so I thought."

You see, what seemed like an extremely basic strategy to me at the time was actually a veil for an extremely extensive and purposeful strategy. I asked her how they decided on that particular strategy, and Rowe told me I was asking her the wrong question.

She said, "Ask me *why*."

With a one word question, that veil disappeared, and that seemingly simple marketing strategy unlocked my mind and opened a three-dimensional view of marketing.

In short, there was a reason why for every step —down to the letter—was based on human psychology and humanitarian impact. Every fathomable ripple was, and is, considered for every component in Rivvly's marketing strategy, PLUS it's adaptable. That strategy only becomes possible when you KNOW YOUR NICHE.

Results

Rivvly's success in targeting a niche market and employing a purposeful marketing strategy to communicate with their audience has not only fueled their ability to grow and reach breakeven in their first year of business, but also organically curated an impressive brand loyalty that resulted in 100 percent year-to-year growth in recurring revenue based soley on referrals. After adding a sales team and dedicated marketing budget the following year, Rivvly is now secured as the industry leader for premier virtual assistants in a matter of 2.5 years.

WHATS THE RESEARCH SAY>

"Start by considering what you offer and what you're good at. The best niche marketing strategies play into your brand's unique strengths and perspectives. So reflect on the special and exceptional qualities of your brand, team, and offerings."[1]

Take UNTUCKit. The company focuses on selling casual shirts that are designed not to be tucked into pants. The idea started in February of 2011 when Chris Riccobono came up with the idea for UNTUCKit while working at GE Healthcare .

He then brought on Aaron Sanandres, a Columbia Business School classmate, to help develop the idea into a business. "The commercial clothing industry is a vertical that can feel like everything has been done. But UNTUCKit proves there are still creative ways to create a new space in a long-established market segment."[2] By making even just a small change, you can build a whole new sector in a traditional space. UNTUCKit probably wasn't looking to create a new type of shirt. They were more likely focused on serving a specific community of people: those who didn't like to tuck in their shirts. To give those people want they wanted, UNTUCKit created a new line of products that solved a problem that a lot of people were having, but didn't know how to solve.

Find a focused niche, figure out their pain points, and tell the story the product's key benefit to the world.

MY STORY OF THE PRINCIPLE

I thought it was almost impossible to stand out in business—really, I thought you had to have millions of dollars. After learning about niches and ways to market inside of them, I was starstruck with the possibilities one can have. For instance, I launched a marketing company but instead of catering to everyone I decided to only focus on a niche.

I was going to do marketing and branding to only C-level executives and founders of organizations. I further carved out a niche by offering personal and professional brand management as the core of the business. I had a narrow audience and an even narrower set of services. My choice is only one avenue a person can take. With the Internet at your fingertips, you have the chance to market to any niche and at scale. This principle is an excellent one to perfect because most people like you don't have millions of dollars to use for your marketing efforts. Thus, a niche enables you to spend your time and money effectively.

ACTION CHECKLIST

- On top of a paper, write down in what area you are trying to find a niche (marketing campaign, product, service, etc.).

  - Research as many niches within that product, service, or company.

  - As you do this, list out as many solutions as you can.

- Next, figure out their pain points.

  - Search relevant industry terms in the form of hashtags.

  - Read what people are saying and jump into the conversation!

    - Ask questions, and if you can answer a question, do so. Be a human, and through these interactions you will A) gain new fans and B) discover relevant pain points that might have been overlooked.

- Combine the two lists, taking one from each side.

- Find a solution that might work.

- Create a test plan and go test to see if that niche works for you.

- If successful, stick with it; if not, repeat the process.

- Remember, if you ever feel like you have lost your way, make sure to ask yourself two questions:

- What do you do?

- For whom do you do it?

In the next chapter, we will be putting this principle into practice and learning how to market within your niche.

"Don't blow off another's candle for it won't make yours shine brighter."

—JAACHYNMA N.E. AGU

"A strong and enthusiastic niche audience can push a topic into mainstream consciousness with speed and force."

—RACHEL SKLAR

CHAPTER 6

CULTURE ROLE

———

"Your culture is your brand."

—TONY HSIEH

"A logo is not a brand and your role is not what you say, it's what you do."

—ANONYMOUS

ROLE TALK

Why do you choose the shoes you wear, the cars you drive, or the restaurants you dine at?

Because of that brands role in culture.

A traditional meaning of a brand is "a type of product manufactured by a particular company under a particular name."[1] This definition is great and all, but how is it that we all are die-hard fans of specific brands and willing to spend more money on certain products just because of the companies brand? What I discovered was that companies establish themselves in a unique way that enable us, the consumers, to present ourselves in that same unique way to the outside world.

How do you establish yourself in the same way? To have the same brand loyalty as some of the biggest companies in the world, you must understand your role in the culture.

Traditionally, we have viewed well-known brands as something reserved only for the most prominent companies. Think of brands such as AT&T, Google, and Coca-Cola.

"For big companies, brand means reputation, legacy and with a lot of media dollars, an established player in any industry. Big companies have more money to throw at media to put their brands out there."

This concept used to mean that those with the money, even if their product was average, could get their product in front of anyone. Does that mean you and I should just wave the white flag of surrender?

Please don't! While many small companies, brands, and entrepreneurs had to sit on the sidelines before, now the game has changed. Smaller companies, those who do not have massive amounts of marketing dollars, must focus an asset that they have a lot of control over, which is the ability to reframe inside of culture. You will learn from Steve Babcock, the chief creative officer at VaynerMedia, a full-service digital agency built for now. VaynerMedia drives business outcomes via the best in class creative, media, influencer marketing, and everything in between. Steve explains that for small brands, the only way to stand a chance in today's world is to become culturally relevant. Branding for small companies has to revolve around the act of establishing your role in the culture.

This principle can be synthesized down to a straightforward question: what is your role in culture?

MY BUSINESS ALREADY HAS A ROLE?

Let's deconstruct this question to help you understand your role in the culture. For most of us, this question is something we don't spend enough time thinking about. Yet it is one of the most important keys to success in a world dominated by brands.

As Steve explains, "Little brands can often feel intimidated because many of them believe they have to go toe to toe with companies like Apple, Nike or Coca-Cola but this is when you have to find a unique culture." As we can see, trying to go head-on with one of these giants is a death sentence, unless you play a different game.

Most business owners think of brand as what business offering they have. For an owner of a pizza shop, the offering may be great pizzas at affordable prices. That is not enough—that is precisely what the other guys are selling. Every person in town is trying to convince you and me they have the best pizzas at affordable prices.

If everyone has the same message, how do you stand out? We already learned that brand is important, so how do you show it?

By defining what your role in that culture is!

Take the example of a local pizza shop in a small town in New Jersey. The pizza shop is not the only restaurant in the state, nor is the only one that serves pizza. The pizza shop is not the biggest or the cheapest, so how does it stand out amid its competitors?

By having a specific role in its communities culture.

You see, the pizza shop derives its power not from its massive marketing budget (because let's be real—if you had all the money in the world, you would just run as much money as you can on advertisements), but from its position in the community.

While its competitors strive to lower prices and expand to more significant segments of New Jersey; the pizza shop only focuses on being right here in the small community. Finding out who you are and who you serve will help you better understand how to go about creating a brand that fits into that community. When we ask the pizza shop owner this question "What is your role is in culture?", it's not the best pizza at affordable rates, it is the role of unifier—the ability to bring the community together and to be the unifier of community in this small town.

You have your brand, you know your role, and now you have to create situations that demonstrate what your brand stands for to prove it. Let's create a way to showcase how we bring the community together and why we are the unifier. Without implementation, no one will see you are serious about your role and you will just go back to being another pizza shop.

"Much like the adage goes actions speak louder than words."

DON'T TELL ME, SHOW ME

This part of marketing is where creativity comes into play, and our pizza shop owner has an idea.

"If you are this small pizza shop then every Friday you have community hour whether families, friends and everyone in the community can be together."

The pizza shop can you pull out all of the tables from the restaurant and move them to the nearby park. As part of the community hour, you can offer a special deal, where you can deliver pizzas to the park to bring everyone together who usually wouldn't be together. There can even be a new offering in the form of the community pizza pie, a ten-feet pizza that can be enjoyed by multiple families. All of these actions further speak to your role in culture, and then, over time and through actions like the ones above, you cement your brand as the unifier.

It's not just what you sell, but why you sell it.

FIND YOUR CULTURE AND THEN FIND A WAY TO BE A PART OF THAT.

This principle holds for not just small companies, but for personal brands as well. When I asked Steve about how this would apply to personal branding, he brought up his boss,

Gary Vaynerchuk, and how he has his own culture and a specific role within that culture.

"His role is to push, mentor and get people motivated, especially entrepreneurs. All that he does reflects this role, whether it be in the books he writes or the talks he gives because it's true to him and he lives it day in and day out."

Everyone has parameters for who they are and who they are not. Your role is to find this information out and use it to have a positive impact on the audience or culture in which you serve. Steve, for instance, used this technique when he was in a band. His band would create amazing pieces of music, but big record labels wouldn't pay attention to them unless they had a large following. He built a local audience by finding his role in the culture of Salt Lake City, Utah. Once he dominated locally, and because his offer was filled with quality, then he was able to expand to a much broader population, ultimately gaining attention from much larger record labels.

Roles matter.

Brands who are sincere and provide an offering that is real to people with a specific role in the culture will in turn be cemented into their community. This foundation will leave them ahead of the curve because they have transformed themselves from a something that you can get anywhere into an indispensable brand.

WHATS THE RESEARCH SAY

Few brands have adapted to finding their role in culture as that of Vans. The Van Doren family established Vans in 1966 and had an idea to manufacture footwear to be sold directly to customers. From the start, Vans was focused on enabling creative expression first and foremost. This goal changed in the 1970s; Vans started to be widely adopted by two emerging crazes in Southern California: skateboarding and, to a lesser extent, bicycle motocross (BMX). "This was because these members of these sports and their surrounding cultures were often depicted as unconventional and anti-establishment." [2]

They wanted a brand that would help support this creative expression, and that brand was Vans. "The appeal of Vans to this diverse congregation is perhaps, a deserved culmination of the company ethos and astute marketing."

Both brands and culture are shaped by stories. Humans build a culture—and, by extension, brands—primarily through telling stories. Vans has found its role in culture and committed to its audience in that culture.

MY STORY THE PRINCIPLE:

Understand that we are all part of some type of culture is a principle all marketers have to follow. Apart from the marketing culture, I am part of several others, such as the longboard, entrepreneur, and foodie cultures.

When I discovered the principle of one's role in culture, primarily from Steve Babcock, I began to understand how necessary it was. I set out to apply it to my own life, and what better way to do so than with my personal brand.

I decided that marketing was for me, and I wanted to focus on increasing my authority on the marketing industry. This battle was fierce because not only were there many other marketers, but there were also those marketers who had way more experience and degrees than I did.

I then decided to take a different approach and began to separate myself from what other marketers did and focus on establishing my role differently in the culture. My part was an educator in the marketing culture, one who focuses on effective marketing in the form of scalable, low-cost and high yield marketing. Establishing this image took a fair amount of trial and error, until I understood that I was not selling my marketing; I was selling practicality and time. I wanted to make marketing as simple and practical as possible because that was the role I wanted to play in the culture. I decided to create white papers and content that would educate people about practical marketing. This book is just another way I aim to fulfill the role I set out to create.

ACTION CHECKLIST

- Grab a blank piece of paper and title this section "My role in culture is____."

- List out the five biggest competitors in your industry in the middle of the page.

- Then, research and write down three things that separate you from all five companies.

- Circle the similar statements that you have written out.

- Synthesize what you circled in less than five words.

- Turn the page and finish the sentence "My role in culture is_____" with those words.

- Now that you know your role, ask your community, staff, friends, and family to brainstorm ways showcase this role.

- If you are not happy, repeat this exercise with a new set of competitors.

"You can never go wrong by investing in communities and the human beings within them."

—PAM MOORE

CHAPTER 7

ATTENTION

"Whatever you focus your attention on will become important to you even if it's unimportant."

—SONYA PARKER

"We're living at a time when attention is the new currency."

—PETE CASHMORE

TIME WELL SPENT

Where do you spend most of your time? Most likely at school, work, with friends, or possibly online. OK, le"s be honest, we probably spend more time online than we are comfortable sharing because that is just where our attention gravitates toward. The internet has made it so easy to be entertained, and we go there at the slightest sign of boredom.

Social platforms such as Facebook, Instagram, LinkedIn, Twitter, YouTube, and so many more garner our attention because we get to consume the type of content we want, on our own time. The same used to be true for television, and before that the radio, but the advent of the Internet enabled attention to be spread wider, and thus more scattered, than before.

However, though this scattering might seem like a bad thing, it has opened up the opportunity for you to leverage it to your advantage. Just ask Gary Vaynerchuck, the CEO of Vaynermedia.

Gary will help teach you how to find the attention of our end users, customers, and audience.

Attention is critical for success in the new game. If no one knows you exist, how can they be a consumer? Much like the tree in the forest, if it falls and no one is around, did it really fall? The same goes for attention of your brand.

Gary and his company pride themselves on understanding the ins and outs of where people spend their time. Here is where the opportunity lies. Opportunities such as this one don't come as frequently as some may hope, therefore it's imperative to capitalize on it when it arrives. Gary perfectly explained at a Keynote presentation he gave in Auckland, New Zealand, where he said, "If you had the opportunity to buy beachfront property for pennies on the dollar, would you do it? The current state of the internet is providing so much opportunity regardless of your ambition...And so many of you aren't taking advantage of the 'underpriced' attention that's available."[1]

Gary has been noted for saying, "For a consumer to get excited about something, to be compelled by something, it comes down to attention. Attention, not impressions. They need to really consume it. That is the game."[2] Attention and getting it has been on the forefront of Gary's mind from an early age, since the days of his first company. Why? Because he understood that if the right people knew where his lemonade stands were, he would earn more sales.

ATTENTION MATTERS

After graduating from college, Gary made his way back to New Jersey to his family's liquor store and took over operations. Part of running the business was to market the company to reach new customers who would in turn bring in more profit for the company. While most in the industry were content with using traditional marketing avenues such as newspaper, radio, and TV advertisements, Gary had something else in mind. He wanted to do something that would move the needle for his business.

Much like Gary, you are looking for different and effective ways to maximize the resources. Low cost, high yield ways to impact your bottom line. What is that resource? The Internet.

While in college, Gary became interested in the Internet and quickly understood that it would be big. He also understood that the platforms built on top of the Internet would be game changers. It wasn't because he was any more technically inclined that you and I are. He just understood that here, on this platform called the Internet, people would spend their time, a.k.a. their attention.

Gary believed in this idea so much so that he set out to create one of the first e-commerce wine businesses in America, winelibrary.com, and built that company on the back of email marketing and Google AdWords using one core principle: pay attention to where users spend their time and deploy the appropriate marketing there.

One of his most successful bets was in Google. Gary was very attentive to where people were spending their time and began to see more people using the platform.

Google had, in fact, become one of the most powerful search engines, and at the tail end of 2000, it released its advertising product, Google AdWords. AdWords works by enabling marketers and advertisers to bid on specific keywords for their clickable ads to appear in Google's search results. At the time, Google was processing roughly eighteen million search queries a day, which, as Gary saw it, meant people were spending their time and attention on this website. [3]

"I was able to grow the business from $3 million to $60 million in revenue ridiculously fast on the back of Google AdWords. I bought broad keywords like "wine" for pennies per click." [4]

The words would start at pennies and slowly bid higher over time, but for months, no one tried to outbid him. In the meantime, Gary was seeing conversions higher than he had ever seen before, in part because he fundamentally understood that the end users' attention was on this new attention rich platform.

He would continue on this trajectory for months, and while others were skeptical, the results spoke for themselves. Today, Google is no longer the undervalued bargain it once was. As its popularity grew, so did the use of its ad product, which in turn raised prices to appropriate levels. Along with the price increase, users started getting used to the advertisements, and therefore began to engage with them less. When asked about this product today, Gary recounts that it's still a good product, except now it's much more expensive and half as effective. He had entered the attention market of Google at its sweet spot, where attention was high, and the advertisements on it were low.

Though the days of cheap ads and high conversions on Google are long gone, the fact remains that there are always alternatives that might be underpriced home runs for you. These alternate platforms constantly change, and, for you to get the most value, experimentation will have to become habitual. Users' attention flows like water, never really staying in one place for too long. However, the leverage still lies in that divided attention.

"No company has had an eternal monopoly on attention and I promise you things will change. You just have to accept that change and be open to storytelling on the mediums of the moment," Gary said. [5]

Gary has learned to embrace this principle. While others are doubting the viability of what's new, he is working hard to produce relevant content on the platforms that users are on. That is why it matters to you.

The best advice he offers is not to be romantic about what worked yesterday, and instead pay attention to what is happening at the moment. Also, he stresses that though the platforms change the fundamentals of audio, video and text do not. These media for content distribution are the framework that humans communicate on and it's your job to understand what you excel at and what your audience wants.

Different populations want different types of content and traverse to one platform of the next. Remember the chapter about understanding your niche? The community with which you want to engage might live on different platforms, so it is critical to understand where your intended audience is.

"We are all in a very basic game of gathering attention. We must gain attention first before we can story-tell how 'savage' we are. If you don't have someone's attention, you've lost." [6]

WHATS THE RESEARCH SAY?

Thales Teixeira is a professor at Harvard Business School whose research revolves around the marketing principles of buying, selling, capturing, and using consumer attention efficiently. [7]

If you aren't familiar with the concept of the attention economy, it's based on the fact that consumer attention is limited and always comes at a price — that price has skyrocketed in recent years. Every single day, there are more companies, with more brands and more products to advertise, which means there's more demand for consumer attention than ever. The problem is, the supply of consumer attention simply hasn't kept pace with this demand: There's no evidence individual human attention capacity is growing. Nor has the population grown as fast as the number of brands has.

Let there be no misunderstanding, ad effectiveness is not down across the board — only when it comes to mass, traditional media, which doesn't hold attention like it used to. But, all is not lost. People do still pay attention — under the right conditions — and there are proven ways to capture that attention more efficiently.

He shares three massive tips to help business navigate:

1. Buy right: Stop wasting money on "spray and pray" media.

2. Maximize attention by optimizing the creative factors you can control.

3. Build up customer attention over the long run.

"There's no magic formula for earning a potential customer's attention, but there are certain principles brands can lean on. Are you spending on the right platforms, and are you leveraging the tools of each in a way that will help you capture and keep consumer attention? Answer that honestly, and you'll be on your way to a fairer fight," Teixera said.[8]

MY STORY OF THE PRINCIPLE:

I learned this principle the hard way, and that is why I really wanted to elaborate on this principle. In early 2018, I started to get serious about my personal brand and decided I would go about actually putting in the time and resources to make it successful. At this time, I made the first mistake: I jumped in and decided to use the one platform I was the most comfortable with, which was Instagram. I made videos, wrote amazing text, and showed up every day, but with little traction. I couldn't understand why. Was I not good enough? Did my message not matter?

I struggled for months and was at the point of stopping the whole operation. Then came the interview with Mark Metry. As we finished the interview, he mentioned that I should switch to LinkedIn for content. I hadn't considered it but decided why not give it a try. I was shocked—on this new platform, I saw similar content creators and a massive base of people who wanted to know what I had to say. I found my target population's attention wasn't on Instagram, but on LinkedIn. Without attention, I got little traction and started to lose faith in my abilities. Little did I know I was in the wrong place with the wrong content. Attention saved me, and by learning to pay close attention, I have grown both as a brand and a marketer.

Do overlook attention.

ACTION CHECKLIST

- First ask, "Where are my target populations?"

    - Do research. Remember Google is your best friend.

    - Find out what platforms your competitors are on and if they are reaching your desired population. They may have done the work for you.

- Learn how to communicate on that platform. Test content to see if your audience pays attention to it,

- You will soon understand that each platform has all three elements of

    - Text

    - Audio

    - Video

- Test as much as you can; in this manner, you will find what speaks to your community.

- Continue to provide value and intent to the target population.

- Become imbedded in the community; that will ensure that when platforms change, you change with that population.

"Attention is a limited resource, so pay attention to where you pay attention."

—HOWARD RHEINGOLD

CHAPTER 8

END IT

———

"A dream becomes a goal when action is taken toward its achievement."

—BO BENNETT

"All successful people have a goal. No one can get anywhere unless he knows where he wants to go and what he wants to be or do."

—NORMAN VINCENT PEALE

WHAT'S THE POINT?

Why do you pay to go to the gym?

We don't need gyms to get into shape; for hundreds of years, there were no gyms and people were just fine. Why, then, do so many people have gym memberships?

Is it because the gym had the nicest equipment, or because it has an Olympic swimming pool? Is it because it was the cheapest one, or because it is the most hip one in the city? If you're like me, then all that was nice, but it wasn't the reason I was there.

We all have the desired outcomes toward which we strive. Whether it is to be a thought leader in your industry, an expert in a particular subject, the best salesperson in your company, a successful business owner, or an effective coach, there is a series of steps and tools that we must go through to get to that outcome.

I learned this principle from Wendy Stevens. Wendy is a celebrated marketer, speaker, and author of numerous best-selling books, but before all that, she was a coach. Before marketing, Wendy was a successful lacrosse player at the University of Maryland and later took that same passion for the game to her role as the first women's Division One head coach of lacrosse at Vanderbilt University.

FOLLOW THE NORTH STAR

Being a coach has tremendously affected the way she markets and is the reason we are going to learn the principle of starting at the end with her.

"I have a background as an athlete, and I have always looked for the clever strategies and tactics to give a competitive advantage to my team."

On the field, this strategy proved to be effective: only two years coaching took her team to become nationally-ranked top twenty. What made her so compelling and effective? She had a clear goal in mind. This strategy would later be put to the test when a series of unfortunate life events left her searching for some way to be at home full time to take care of her children. She decided she would use the skills she had developed while being a coach to launch a company of her own.[1]

"This was a challenge because up to this point I had had no prior marketing or business experiences, the only advantage I had was that I had been a communications major in college," Wendy said.

This challenge didn't deter her at all. She had a clear goal in mind: to take care of her family.

Marketing is always changing; strategies that work today might not work tomorrow. This constant fluctuation can be frustrating—you might spend a lot of resources on a campaign just to find out that your competitor already did it or that no one is on that platform anymore. As all this happens, you and your team will need a North Star to look at.

The North Star for marketing is a specific goal, and having a goal in mind even before you start will ensure that your marketing is always aligned with your goal.

THE STAR

Wendy had her goal, and, with it in mind, she set off and decided to work backward to find a way to make it happen. With limited resources by her side, she had to learn how to become more resourceful. By looking for ways to be effective with limited resources, she kept at it, knowing her big break was just around the corner.

As mentioned in the story of Gary Vaynerchuck, Google AdWords was released in the early 2000s, and Wendy "was quick to see this fantastic opportunity. I even attended one of the very first training that Google AdWords and would become one of the first 200 Google certified Adwords specialists in October of 2000."

"Internet marketing in the early days was difficult because it was so new." Her situation totally changed one morning at 2 a.m. She was setting up a new campaign but because of lack of sleep and one particularly bad training session recently, in which she got her "butt kicked," she was not paying too much attention. She brushed over some critical steps: she selected the wrong setting for where her ads would run and she failed to set a bid limit. The first mistake she made was accidentally choosing the content network instead of the search network.

"Search network shows ads when a user is a search for something, while the content network shows ads inside of actual websites." Her second mistake was forgetting to set up a bid limit for her AdWords. The combination of these two mistakes was eye-opening. In less than forty-five minutes, her credit card was charged $10,000. Though this was a shock at first, it turned out to be a blessing. Because she had brushed over some of these details, "I ended up generating leads under a $1, some as low as 50 cents a lead which before this it would cost me closer to $40 a lead."

The tables had turned, and these experiences were a wake-up call and would become the framework of her book, *Reverse Google Marketing.*

She detailed the strategy she developed after this accident when she was marketing with AdWords. One common theme she saw with this campaign and many like it was that it really only worked because she had mastered the basics. She said,

I started a campaign not worrying about the numbers, but what I wanted the outcome of this specific campaign to be.

My dumb, blind luck is that I bumped into not one but two of the top internet marketers in the country. One of whom did the marketing for Kevin Harrington, the founder of As Seen On TV and celebrity guest for the televised show shark tank. I got a world-class education from that gentleman and others that lead me to have a best seller on Amazon called *Reverse Google Marketing.*

"OUTCOMES MATTER"

To run a successful campaign, or any marketing effort for that matter, you have to determine precisely who is the target audience you are trying to reach and how to speak to them, which is what we discovered in previous chapters. When this part is done, you want to reverse engineer the goal you want to accomplish from this particular campaign. Wendy found that having a clear outcome, whether in sports or marketing, was imperative for success.

Using the principle of outcome marketing tactics, she jumped into her first significant company launch with two business partners called the Google reverse funnel system. Over the next five years, she ran $146 million worth of marketing campaigns, and the success of each campaign was due to the goal having been set before the campaign was even started.

What does this mean for you?

You want to find the most significant pain or problem. This search is important because you only want to create a hook for the most significant pain point the potential client has and then create the right content so you can explain what's in it for them.

"You want a marketing plan that doesn't focus on selling the product but rather the outcome of that product or service."

Take the example of gym memberships we mentioned above. So often, people will go to a gym, and the salesperson will go on and on talking about the details of the gym. The seven thousand-square foot gym is open 24/7, but these details are not what is most essential. The most critical thing is the outcome: the feeling of getting healthy, looking great, and feeling good. Selling the outcome is really what everyone wants. Plenty of people don't want to go to the gym—they want to be buff and feel beautiful in their bodies, but they are willing to buy this membership because of the feeling that it will give them.

I go there to lose fat and gain muscle because I have an outcome in mind and a gym is just a tool of helping me get closer to my desired outcome. I only care about how close that particular gym could get me to my desired outcome.

- You always have to ask yourself the question when you are creating a campaign, creating your copy, or doing anything within your marketing efforts: so what?

- Why does that particular piece or image or landing page matter?

- Does it talk about the outcome or what they want?

If it does talk about the outcome, then you are much more likely to have a successful campaign. If it doesn't, you will miss the mark and lead a campaign that will ultimately be unsuccessful. Learn to run your marketing by focusing on your target audience, create messages that speak to them and never try to sell the product and its features.

Focus on the outcome that such a product will give your audience.

WHATS THE RESEARCH SAY

Tim Ferriss, a well-known author and entrepreneur, wanted to create a book that would have a massive impact on society at large. His goal was for *4-Hour Workweek* to be the go-to resource for an overworked employee or an entrepreneur trapped in their own business. Tim's intent was for his book to serve as a compass for a new and revolutionary world. Armed with this ambitious goal, he set off to find out what his audience wanted and further create content that would practical for his them. With this in mind, he developed a vision that his target market desired, followed by concrete plans to implement ways to achieve it. His vision hit home for many because the message didn't stop at "work harder" like in other books.[2]

Instead, this book was about working smarter and enjoying life along the way. When the book was completed, the market was primed for it because it was written for them. Tim didn't rely on their own beliefs or assumptions to guide his decisions. He set course to test everything along the way. *4-Hour Workweek* was a smash hit based on the data that was gathered along the way. Tim would take the same principle into building a story around the book by engaging with his audience on social media. The use of social media would help build energy behind the book, increase word of mouth marketing, and create a movement that would ultimately lead to over a million copies of the book being sold.

MY STORY OF THE PRINCIPLE:

I wanted to establish myself as a marketer and thought leader in digital marketing—an ambitious goal, but I was sure I could do it. Knowing the goal was to be a marketer, I decided to create content that would be valuable and insightful for those in the marketing field, as well as those who were just getting started in the field. One strategy was to associate with other marketers in my niche, through both creating collaborative opportunities and by becoming friends with them.

I actually wanted these friendships because I knew I could learn as much from them as they could from me. These steps were complemented by creating specific content on social platforms to allow me to share my expertise. I used mostly LinkedIn, where a good majority of my content was centered around marketing. Because I had that end goal, I created a road map and action items to help lead me into the direction of my goal.

ACTION CHECKLIST

- Make sure you have completed the previous chapters in finding your niche, understanding your role in culture, and learning about where your audience 's attention lies. Once you have completed them, you are ready to get started with this checklist.

- For each campaign, marketing strategy, or piece of content, get a piece of paper or word document and split it in half.

- Write down at the top of one side MY OUTCOME and on the other side CUSTOMER OUTCOME.

- Next, define what your outcome is; try to make it more precise than "increase brand awareness" or "increase sales."

- Do the same for the customer. What do they really want the outcome to be from what you offer?

- This exercise will give you a framework and a tool to ground you when you are marketing. It will keep it clear what your intention is and why does it matter to your customer.

Goal: Understand how to apply the desired outcome to your marketing strategy as a tool to better connect with your audience.

"If you set goals and go after them with all the determination you can muster, your gifts will take you places that will amaze you."

—LES BROWN

"Stay focused, go after your dreams, and keep moving toward your goals"

—LL COOL J

CHAPTER 9

MESSAGE IT

"Whenever you want to achieve something, keep your eyes open, concentrate and make sure you know exactly what it is you want. No one can hit their target with their eyes closed."

—PAULO COELHO

"Concentrate all your thoughts upon the work at hand. The sun's rays do not burn until brought to a focus."

—ALEXANDER GRAHAM BELL

IPOD'S DIRTY SECRET

I have a feeling not many of us are rushing to call customer support, right? Calling customer support evokes about the same level of excitement as sitting in traffic or being stuck in bed with an extreme cold. We know it's going to be time intensive and, most likely, we are going to receive some sort of unfavorable news. A young man had this exact experience in 2003 when he was calling Apple about his battery dying for his iPod touch. Because the item was eighteen months old, Apple gave him two options

Option One: Pay a ridiculously high price for its repair.

Option Two: Just get a new one.

What would you do in that situation? Many of us would hang up, upset, and proceed to either buy a new one or not, but not Casey Neistat.

Casey, age twenty-two at the time, was frustrated about his iPod's battery life decided to create a third option: he created a video called "iPod's Dirty Secret." The video shows Casey spray painting "iPod's Unreplaceable Battery Lasts Only 18 Months," after getting off the phone with a customer support agent. To serve as a public service announcement, he targets iPod posters in Manhattan, spraying each Apple advertisement all to the soundtrack of rap group N.W.A.'s song "Express Yourself." [1]

The message is clear, simple, and was viewed more than six million times within the first month of its release in 2003. As you might expect, Casey was propelled into mainstream media.

Since then, he has become a well-known YouTube personality, a recognized filmmaker with work that has been featured on HBO, a vlogger, and cofounder of a video sharing platform company that was acquired by CNN. [2]

Even if you aren't producing documentaries or feature films, it is still impressive to see a man reach such extraordinary heights with no formal training. I want Casey to teach you a principle that has aided in his success, focusing on the message.

WE ARE ROLLING

From very humble beginnings. Casey strived to become a film producer and find a way to break into the industry. Not having any connections or leads, he tried to do it with the help of his older brother, two video cameras, and few computers for editing. The pair moved to New York City and set out to create short films and commercials, anything to get experience and notoriety. They had early success with films like "iPod's Dirty Secret" and a few more short films, but real success would come a few years later. [3]

Until then Casey would focus on his craft, experimenting as much as he could and refining his storytelling all in anticipation for what was about to come.

His big break would come in 2008.

Casey had amassed a good amount of content they had filmed and decided package up a few of episodes into a series called "The Neistat brothers." They took the series and pitched it to TV networks.

After a few pitches, he found some interest and eventually was able to sell the show to HBO in 2008 for just under $2 million.[4] It would take a full three years for the show to appear, and, in the meantime, Casey went through a rough patch.

This outlet would come in the form of creating a YouTube channel called "Casey Neistat."

"TRY AND TRY AGAIN"

Casey's redemption would come after getting a parking ticket for riding his bike on the sidewalk and not the designated bike lane in New York City. This ticket frustrated him because of all the obstructions in the bike lane, and he decided that, with a friend, he would create a video about how the bike lane is impossible it is to use.

The footage showed him riding his bike in the bike lane, but, rather than moving outside of the bike lane to avoid obstacles, he would merely run into them. It turned out to be utterly hilarious because he would run into traffic cones, trucks, and, most famously, a police officer's car. The point of the video was that it is difficult to follow the rules of using the bike lane because of all the barriers that are presented.[5]

Casey had once again found a way to create a piece of content that had a compelling message with a funny twist that was heard. Though he had multiple viral hits prior to this one, with the advent of YouTube, companies started to see the value that vitality had on brands as a marketing tool. Brands started to understand that videos such as the one Casey created, which showcased a simple message, had the potential to enact real change and so soon after the video went viral Casey was contacted by *The New York Times*.

They asked him to create video content for them. This publicity would further elevate him to new heights, all based on the premise of making creative videos with messages that are memorable because of their simplicity.

Casey understood that the message you put out is much more important than the production quality of the video.

"People can forgive lower quality work as long as there is a message that is compelling and meaningful," he said. [6]

Take his work with Nike, for instance. Casey was employed to create three videos that would serve as the cornerstone of Nike's campaign launch of their new FuelBand. He created two great commercials but wanted to do something completely different with the last one.

"I didn't want to make crappy TV commercials I wanted to create something I believed in. I had made the past two videos [for Nike] that I liked but it came time to make the third video. So I called my editor, who was one of my closest friends for an adventure," Casey said. [7]

He set out to use a massive amount of the Nike campaign's budget and on a ten-day world trip around the world. From this trip, he crafted a story and created a video that to date has exceeded twenty-eight million views on YouTube, making it one of Nike's most watched commercials.

This four and a half-minute video was creatively shot and presented in an easily consumed way that made it an instant hit for both Casey and Nike. The video incorporates humor and other interesting elements, but the real reason for its success is its focus on the message.[8]

In this case, Casey focused on #makeitcount and showed how it pertained to him and his love for adventure, travel, and challenging the norm. The trip took him from New York to places like Paris, Cairo, London, Johannesburg, and Bangkok. He then connected the trip to the campaign by explaining the message of how Nike products empower him to pursue adventure.

We like to focus on the quality of the work we put out, which is still really important, but we let this focus on quality overshadow the real point we are trying to make: the message.

The message, whether in a video, audio, or in text, is why people will pay attention to you. It's the message that really speaks to us. You should learn to ask

- Why you are creating this content?

- What is the overall message that we want people to walk away with?

The power lies in the answers to these questions lies; knowing that information will enable you to create content that evokes a specific feeling and compels the consumer to take action.

In each of the stories above, Casey focused on effectively expressing his message. He first tried to understand the message he was trying to convey to his audience. Then he was free to experiment and build creative content around the message. His story perfectly demonstrates that to get attention today, the key is to create a message with meaning behind it.

Knowing this principle is an opportunity for you: while everyone else is focusing on nuances that really don't matter, you know the advantage is to focus on what does matter—in this case, your message.

WHATS THE RESEARCH SAY?

Lush also realized the need to get their message out in as big a way as possible.

> The 'ethical cosmetics' company has gone from starting out with a small cult following, to being a retail behemoth in recent years. With latest figures putting **total turnover at \$1.3 billion** for the year to June 2017. And the best part? Lush have done it all having spent *next to nothing* on traditional, mainstream advertising.
>
> Core values are at the epi-centre of every single thing Lush does. For them, it's not about selling bath products and lipstick. It's about **trying to revolutionize**

an industry that they feel is doing things in an unsustainable way—they started with why.

Lush's word-of-mouth marketing strategy is successful because it has these clear values at its core. They **stand for something** that aligns with a lot of other people's values—and then sell products off the back of it. And they focus a lot on that connection with their content.

But what Lush have done is **created masses of conversations** about topics that are important to them and align with their brand values. Garnering a following of like-minded people in a way that provides a logical link back to their products. [9]

In other words: People engage with, love and share Lush's content. And this, in turn, spreads word-of-mouth about their message and mission in order to generate sales and build a community that encourages engagement. But the key to it all stems from how clear and well-aligned Lush are to their company values. They stand for something big and create content that's around that—evoking an emotional response in their followers and customers. (Galera, R. "How Lush Cosmetics Hit Billion-dollar Revenues with Word-of-Mouth Marketing - Word-of-Mouth and Referral Marketing Blog.")

MY STORY OF THE PRINCIPLE

I have seen this principle overlooked so many times, by marketers and businesses alike. Yet it is a principle that has served me extraordinarily well. For instance, I received little to no traction when I started my brand. I attribute this completely to my messaging. I was too scattered, trying to talk about any and everything I could. This disorganization confused my audience, and, for that, I was unable to build a community. My strategy completely changed when I understood that every successful brand, from the biggest to the smallest, focuses on their messaging.

For companies like Lush, it is focusing on the message of selling and supporting cruelty-free products—products that have not been tested on animals. This message in one the company lives and stands by, a dissolve message. For me, I have created a brand about clear cut, practical marketing, marketing that is to the point and that anyone can learn with hard work and dedication.

ACTION CHECKLIST

- For this checklist, refer back to the chapter with Wendy Stevens. Gather your sheet with desired outcomes for you and your customer. This sheet will act as reference to help you craft your message.

- Take your outcome and under both sections, list out up to five bullet points.

- In each of the two sections, your outcome and the customer outcome, start to list out phrases or messages that you would want to convey.

- For you, list out phrases that you would want someone to say about you or your organization.

- For your customer, list out what they say about you now.

- Refer back to the desired outcomes because ones message should be aligned to the outcome.

- For example, if you want your customers outcome to be "feels safer," your messages should be in line with that, such as "this company/product/service makes it a point to there for their customers through thick and thin."

- Continue to iterate and test the message. Testing will be discussed more in the chapter about analytics.

"My success, part of it certainly, is that I have focused in on a few things."

—BILL GATES

CHAPTER 10

BE PERENNIAL

———

*"The work that lasts over time is the work which still speaks
to us when all contemporary interest in that work is extinct."*
—JEANETTE WINTERSON

There are two doors in front of you:

- One will give you a $10 today, right now (I bet you didn't think
  this book would make you that much money right off the bat).

- The other will give you $200 paid in $50 increments over
  the next year.

Which door do you choose? The answer probably depends
on what your current needs are, but, most likely, you will

pick the larger sum over time, right? It's more money, you just have to wait a little longer. Well, this same game can be applied to content creation. In marketing, we have this term called Evergreen content.

Webster (W) defines evergreen as:

a: retaining freshness or interest : PERENNIAL

b: universally and continually relevant : not limited in applicability to a particular event or date[1]

In normal words, evergreen content is always relevant and does not become dated. Evergreen or perennial content is equivalent to Door Two from the above example.

"THE PERENNIAL SELLER"

Ryan Holiday is a marketer, entrepreneur, and *New York Times* best-selling author who has written six books before the age of thirty. Ryan began his career by dropping out of college at age nineteen and after dropping out found himself working for one of the most successful authors today, Robert Greene. Ryan has written extensively about marketing and always has an interesting opinion. After the release of his book *Perennial Seller: The Art of Making and Marketing Work that Lasts*, I knew he had struck gold—gold I want him to share with you.[2]

MAKE IT LAST

One of Ryan's biggest passions has always been writing, but as he mentioned on a #ASKGARYVEE interview:

"I was never one of those kids that always wanted to write, I think I just fell in love with books," Ryan said.

He didn't get into writing until he worked with Robert Greene, and from that moment on, he saw it was possible to make a living writing about topics you are passionate about.

"I wanted to create content that makes an impact and what I am excited about." He loved the idea that a person can take something that he is fascinated in and make it consumer friendly and exciting to an audience that might not have expected to be interested in that type of topic.

The idea stuck with him, and later on, in his twenties, he was the director of marketing for American Apparel, which at that time was one of the largest fashion brands in the United States. One idea kept populating his mind: creating content that lasts. Take a video, for instance. It takes the same amount of work to create a video on YouTube about a breaking news story as it does to create one about how to emotionally connect with your audience successfully. They both take hours research, filming, and editing.

Which will last longer?

The news story might get one thousand views in a day, but what about in a year from now—will that video ever be watched again? One that emotionally connects with your audience might receive ten views at the end of the first day, but within a year, that number could reach five thousand and continue to attract interest years down the road. This idea directly influences how we should think of marketing; so much focus has been put on what's new and trendy rather than focusing on what has made successful brands and marketing last.

This principle is based on a premise called the Lindy effect. "[The Lindy Effect] says that for every year that you are in business or for every year that your work exists, its half-life decreases by one year. If your brand has been around for ten years, most likely it would take 20 years for no one to forget your brand altogether." [3]

The focus should be placed on creating something that becomes a perennial seller, which is something that continues to sell and be relevant, well after the sales and attention cycle stop. It's hard to create a product, service, or marketing materials, so why don't we create something that lasts?

This principle boils down to putting in the effort, dedication, and hard work that will lead to the success you envision. To begin, you have first to have to answer this question:

- Is the marketing you are putting together actually going to be relevant now as well as a few years from now?

BRAND INTEREST

Where do we start?

"You want to study classical works in marketing and history to find whats familiar in them. Then root your work into these larger ideas, not what the current landscape is favoring," Ryan said.[4]

"We have this bias towards newness because that's what's exciting but the truths the vast majority of revenue or interest comes from the established so called classics. Like Jeff Bezos, who's the founder of Amazon, has this great rule that says focus on the things that don't change. People always want cheap stuff and they always want it right away. Those are the core principles of Amazon," Ryan said.[5]

This understanding is critical because these larger ideas have stood the test of time for a reason. If you take the easy route or take shortcuts, you are going to make something that is more closely related to a fad and is not going to stand the test of time.

For example, consider the time Ryan worked at American Apparel. The company made timeless classics in the form of socks, T-shirts, hoodies, and so forth, totaling fifty million garments sold a year worth over a billion dollars. The CEO, however, started to see that his competitors were doing exceptionally well, with more stylish apparel, while his company was focused on more of the timeless pieces. Instead of remaining true to the company's roots, he decided to change the whole business model to focus on copying his competitor's trendy articles of clothing.

At first, this endeavor went well, but as time went on and he created trendy, fashionable clothing that didn't sell, the company started to drown in its inventory every season. The one billion dollar company was later sold for only sixty million dollars because of bankruptcy.

"The company strayed from its position of being unique and timeless to being trendy which based on its way of doing business spelled disaster for the company," Ryan said.[6] You have to focus on what you are doing and how it can be told in order to create something that lasts.

We often look at our competitors' marketing or that of people who are doing something similar to us and try and use it as a reference point to see how we are doing comparatively. This tactic is a massive mistake.

"Though it is good to have an idea what your competitors are doing, it is unwise to follow their lead blindly," Ryan said. [7]

Those people might have different missions or spending ability than you or run a bad business. Thus, following them will lead you astray. "We have to root ourselves in the principles that we know are important to our brand and stick to that." The best reference point to which to compare your brand your potential. Take Ryan's friend, Jason Fried, the cofounder of Basecamp, a project management and team communication software company.

CASE STUDY: BASECAMP

Basecamp was doing well and had been in business for over a decade when its competitor Slack came along. The company was faced with the idea of abandoning its principles to do what its competitor was doing. At this point, Slack was getting a lot more attention and investment, so the decision was difficult. Unlike American Apparel, it stayed true to itself. Learn to build a company and marketing that is based on longevity and timelessness because chasing fads will not help you win longterm.

The point is: The first and most essential step of a perennial seller is creating something truly great. As my mentor Robert Greene put it, "It starts by wanting to create a classic." If you're sitting down to make something and thinking about how famous it's going to make you, how rich you're going to get, how fun it's going to be, or all the people you're going to prove wrong, you are thinking about the wrong thing. An essential part of making perennial, lasting work is making sure that you're pursuing the best of your ideas and that they are ideas that only you can have (otherwise, you're dealing with a commodity and not a classic). (Ferriss, T. "How to Create a Perennial Bestseller.")

WHATS THE RESEARCH SAY?

HubSpot Research, which analyzed blogging data from more than fifteen thousand companies, further supports Ryan's principle of creating content that lasts. Evergreen content will have a much greater return than content based on short-term trends or fads.

The researchers recommend to focus on "posts whose traffic grows steadily over time." One must focus on creating content that will still be relevant or of interest to your audience in the future. "These posts are far more valuable than 'decaying' posts, which deliver a surge of traffic and then decay over time. While only one in ten posts are compounding posts, they account for 38% of total blog traffic across our sample."[8]

The research further breaks down the "computed the rate of growth of almost 2,000 compounding and 18,000 decaying posts from top performing business blogs. Based on our analysis, if you publish a compounding blog post in January, you can expect it to receive 2.5 times as many visits per month by July. In contrast, if you publish a decaying blog post in January, by July you will attract less than a fifth of your initial audience."

MY STORY OF THE PRINCIPLE:

Though my research is not as in depth as that of HubSpot Research, I have seen time and again that content focused on Evergreen principles does exponentially better than content focused on fads or short-term topics. This principle is not limited to the written form; both in audio and visual forms, Evergreen content enables me to create meaningful work that has compounding effects. Now, don't get me wrong, I do share short-term content on occasion to keep my brand fresh, but it is only a supplement to my overall content creation strategy.

ACTION CHECKLIST

- Gather all the research you have done from each corresponding chapter's notes.

- Get a new piece of paper.

  - Divide the sheet in half and write "how" or "what" content pieces on each respective side.

- Study the notes you already have and start to think of creating content, video/text/audio, as tactical not topical.

- Content such as this may include

  - Create and maintain a list of blogs in a niche

  - "Everything you need to know" style

  - In-depth case studies or white papers

  - List of free/paid tools

  - Best books for your niche

- Brainstorm five to ten ideas for each of the above points

"If we make anything that lasts, it outlives us."

—JEANETTE WINTERSON

CHAPTER 11

TELL ME A STORY

———

"Marketing is no longer about the stuff that you make but about the stories you tell."

—SETH GODIN

MAMMOTH VS IPHONE

Ever since the dawn of humans, we have been telling stories.

Whether it was telling tales of mammoth hunts during the ice age or mystical dragons in medieval Europe, we love telling stories. This premise holds true throughout history and now into the era of digital media, where effective storytelling can take you and your company to whole new levels.

One person that has learned and truly mastered such story-telling is Jay Shetty.

Jay was born in London, United Kingdom, and from an early age, he was intrigued by why people do the things that they do. This curiosity was the reason he decided to go to Cass Business School in London to study for a degree in behavioral economics. As a business student, he was introduced to successful entrepreneurs and business leaders, who moved him to decide he would follow a similar path, but more focused on investment banking.[1]

While still in his first year, one of his close friends dragged him to a lecture by a monk. Reluctant to go at first, he finally caved and with his friend went to hear this monk speak. Jay was instantly captivated by the message; he would later recall the moment with the monk by saying, "He captivated me like someone I have never seen before, his energy and ora was just infectious." This experience led him to shadow the monk each winter break in India.[2]

Eventually, driven by an inherent desire to help people, Jay dedicated his life to monkhood and for three years spent time as a monk.

"I became a monk because I got fascinated by giving everything you have in the service of others at a very early age," Jay told Lewis Howes in a 2019 interview.

During this time, he would spend upwards of four to eight hours meditating, learning ancient breathing techniques, focusing one's mind, and many other personal development studies. He dedicated the rest of the day to helping others in the local community, from helping harvest crops to teaching.

His real test came in the form of instruction from the elder monk, who had been so much more than a mentor to him. The monk urged Jay to return to London and share the lessons he learned with the world.

Jay was heartbroken.

"I felt like I had failed..but decided to take his advice and go back."

After returning to London, he spent months reintroducing himself to the hustle and bustle of daily living. Though this was challenging, something miraculous started happening. While Jay was away, a lot of his classmates and friends had been working at highly stressful jobs.

Thus, they sought some way to become more mindful and asked Jay to come speak and share stories about ways to deal with stress at their companies.

"I came back in a point in our world that mindfulness, wellbeing and all these things were coming into the corporate workplace."

He started to put his message and storytelling abilities to use, and he slowly gained some momentum from these events. He continued with these events but noticed that within the broader societal trends, mindfulness was becoming a hot topic.

He knew that he was onto something, as his teachings were making such a positive impact on so many individuals.

LET THE STORY BEGIN

In 2013, Jay decided that in order to create a more meaningful impact, he had to understand technology because it was increasingly becoming a part of our everyday world. To integrate technology into his mindfulness practices, he got a job in the technology space to intrench himself in that world. He realized he had a knack for social media, and as he experimented, he started to gain more insight and skill than he could have ever anticipated.

After two years, he decided to take a leap, and in 2015 he quit his job to pursue his passion for helping people through the lessons he learned as a monk, mainly using storytelling. This goal proved difficult because he had no connections in the media world and no one would give him a chance, so with no other options, he turned to YouTube as a way to share his message with the world.

He saw YouTube as a way to create videos and share his messages in a way that would be scalable and not just limited to the corporate arena, where he had only worked up until this point.

Jay started to intentionally establish a clear focus on the purpose of the story. After setting your purpose, you want to focus on creating stories in a way that will enable your audience to be as involved as possible without having to be physically there. You can engage the audience using comments, putting suggestions from past videos in the story, or finding a way to make the audience feel as if they were involved with the creation of the message. The second point he focused on was crowdsourcing his stories, finding out what the audience craved; once he what the audience wanted, he created original content about it.

Because of this strategy, he was able to gain tens of thousands of views on YouTube within a few months. After three months, he finally got the big break when an editor showed Arianna Huffington, the founder of the *Huffington Post*, his content.

She loved Jay's videos.

Huffington and her editor agreed to feature his videos if he could create a series for them. The first of the four videos in the series goes out on the *HuffPost* Facebook page, and, within one week, the video had over a million views. The rest of the videos were released shortly after, and once it was all said and done, Jay's videos had received the most views out of any series *HuffPost* had done.

Jay understood that from the video, he was able to do what he is most passionate about: storytelling. Storytelling, especially over social media, is a way for you and your company to be able to bring together your overarching purpose. These stories are essential because they require generosity from the storyteller; the storyteller has to open up and connect with people on a much deeper level.

We consume information better through stories; harnessing your story gives you a competitive advantage!

WHATS THE RESEARCH SAY

"Many business people have already discovered the power of storytelling," says Paul J. Zak.

Research further supports that storytelling can have a significant effect on the outcome of a business endeavor.

"In a practical sense," continues Zak, "they have observed how compelling a well-constructed narrative can be. But recent scientific work is putting a much finer point on just how stories change our attitudes, beliefs, and behaviors." [3]

Zak and his team aimed to uncover what makes storytelling effective:

- "A story must first sustain attention—a scarce resource in the brain—by developing tension during the narrative.

- If the story is able to create that tension, then it is likely that attentive consumers will come to share the emotions of the characters in it, and after it ends, are likely to continue mimicking the feelings and behaviors of those characters.

- This phenomenon explains the feeling of dominance you have after James Bond saves the world, and your motivation to work out after watching the Spartans fight in *300*.

- When you want to motivate, persuade, or be remembered, start with a story of human struggle and eventual triumph. It will capture people's hearts—by first attracting their brains." [4]

MY STORY THE PRINCIPLE:

Storytelling might seem like something we just loved as children, but when you really look at the lot of content to which you pay attention on a daily basis, much of it is in the form of stories. I struggled with this principle for a while, but, with practice, I started to be able to better craft my message. Storytelling works because it allows us to tap into a person's emotions and connect with them in a meaningful, scalable way. I realized that a story told in the right way can have lasting impacts.

If I asked you to think of one advertisement you saw three weeks ago, what comes to mind? if you're like me, probably nothing! I see so many advertisements each day, how on Earth am I going to remember one from three weeks ago?

Now, let me ask you: what was your favorite movie as a kid?

I bet that one took no time at all. For me, the answer right away was *The Lion King*. This example illustrates the power of storytelling. We are programmed to remember stories because stories that stay with us tend to be meaningful.

Storytelling makes your content much more personable and increases the probability that it will be accepted by your target audience. Learning to craft a story also means that, regardless of changes in technology or social media platforms, you will still be able to know how to communicate with a person in a meaningful way.

- Telling stories is hard wired into us but learning to communicate them to the world can be difficult.

- Get a new piece of paper

  - Separate the page into five sections and title them:

    - **Who you are:** How your company came to exist, and what are your vision, mission, values, and culture?

    - **What you do:** The product or service you provide.

    - **Who you do it for:** The people you want to help.

    - **Why you do it:** Your larger goal; not just what product or service you provide but also how that benefits your customer (e.g., your app helps book vacations so that your customer can truly relax).

    - **How you do it:** Visibility into your product, production, or process.

- **Where you are headed:** How you are evolving and working to create the best product or service for your customers.

  - Spend some time defining all of these because it's important and critical that your vision is properly defined.

  - Now, on a new sheet of paper, list out the brand stories that most resonate with you:

    - List out the companies that most closely remind you of your brand for ten minutes.

    - Hint: they can be outside of your industry.

  - Pick the top three and study the way they present their story.

    - Break the remainder of the page into the three company sections and find content examples from those companies.

- Once you have significant examples, start to replicate the way those stories have been told, keeping in mind how those brands represent themselves in their content.

"'Good story' means something worth telling that the world wants to hear. Finding this is your lonely task. But the love of a good story... and a world driven by your passion, courage and creative gifts is still not enough. Your goal must be a good story well told."

—ROBERT MCKEE

CHAPTER 12

SOCIAL SELLING

———

"The key to a great life lies in shifting your focus from accumulation to contribution. The old saying 'He who gathers the most toys wins' needs to be replaced with 'He who serves the most prospers.' Remember, happiness is the by-product of a life spent adding value to other people's lives."

—ROBIN SHARMA

"Flourishing goes beyond happiness, or satisfaction with life. True, people who flourish are happy. But that's not the half of it. Beyond feeling good, they're also doing good-adding value to the world."

—BARBARA FREDRICKSON

"SOCIAL FIRST SELLING"

We have all been there: we log into our favorite social media app and see a message appear. Instantly, your mind races with the possibilities. Maybe it's a long-lost friend, a client raving how great of a job you are doing, or a past boss begging you to come back for a significantly higher salary. You open up the message.

"Hi or Hi (Your name misspelt)

Are you looking for _____(product that doesn't relate to any of your needs)"

It was just another out of the blue sales pitch. Now, let me ask you, how many of you actually read those messages? If you are like me, you probably delete the message at the first sign of a sales pitch. The same is true in the physical world, too.

You wouldn't go up to a complete stranger in a restaurant and ask them to buy your product or service, right? They might not even need your product, have the money for it, be the decision maker, have context for what you offer, and so on.

You would first get to know them, understand their wants, and see if what you offer is even something that they want. Why does that go away when we go online?

It shouldn't.

How do we break this cycle and learn to put the social back in social media?

Learning to sell through social media is now more imperative than ever, and that is where my friend and published author, Keynote speaker, and National Director of Social Sales at Fidelity National Financial Chelsea Peitz comes along. Much like me, she came into marketing as a way to help her business grow and soon discovered the real potential that digital could have.

"Social is about conversations and communities. The kind that work like the old fashioned meeting in person and getting to know people. It's about getting away from polished guides and getting into unpolished real life. The funny thing is that it probably always was about that, but we got in our own way. We focused on metrics instead of dialogue," Chelsea said.

Before marketing became her life, she studied clinical psychology at Arizona State University, and, after graduating, she decided to go into the real estate business with her husband. The couple saw prosperity in the market all the way up until the recession of 2008. When it hit, Chelsea and her husband lost everything, from the properties that they owned to the investments they had made. "With nothing, we moved back in with our parents and decided with nothing to lose, we would start a fitness company all from scratch."

Chelsea knew nothing about marketing but had to figure out how to market the business in a way that was cost effective and impactful. The first few months seemed to be filled with only frustration, as it became ever more difficult to find clients in the midst of this recession. Her saving grace would come because of social media.

"After seeing some of my contemporaries have early success through social media, I started to get more serious on what it was and how I could use it."

She was instantly hooked, and frankly astounded, because social media marketing had the two elements she needed. Something that had low up-front cost and high effectiveness—exactly what she was looking for. She became determined to become an expert in social media marketing. In this time she found early success and soon "was able to land a prominent role at Fidelity National Financial as their marketing director even though I had done no marketing up until the creation of my company." From that point on, she became fascinated with marketing, especially with the emergence of prominent platforms like Snapchat and Instagram.

"What I learned through trial and error was that I could leverage these platforms to employee a new way of selling known as social selling. Social Selling is the concept of using platforms where people spend most of their time to create relationships and drive sales.

"Social selling is a new buzzword. In plain English, it means using the tools we already use on a daily basis like Facebook, Instagram and Snapchat to create authentic relationships and add value through education or entertainment with a community of people that one day may be a customer," Chelsea said.[1]

Social selling incorporates traditional marketing tactics such as sharing the same contextual information that will help someone better their lives or business. The twist is to go to where every single person spends hours a day on and present yourself in the right way on these media.

THE NOT SO ANNOYING/ KIND OF MY FRIEND SALES PERSON

Let's take the example of the same person who spammed our inbox earlier.

"Those annoying messages where the first message that is sent is promoting products and services. This spam is often met with little effect and general irritation, but there is a way to do social media and branding in a way that is the right way of communication to provide value in a relevant time frame that will attract people," Chelsea said.

This example is where your new method of social selling comes into play. In this manner, you aim to provide value up front and build an authentic relationship.

These elements are key to your social selling strategy:

A) Providing up-front value

B) Being friendly and helpful

C) Being yourself

All of these elements will in turn attract more people to you. The best part of social media is that you can streamline you while keeping it personal.

"You used to need to go to networking events, and at maximum, you could only meet 10-20 people a day before you are out of hours. Now, however, you can reach upwards of 50-100 people a day, and they get to see your face still and have a one-on-one conversation with them," Chelsea said.

The conversation doesn't stop there; those exact people are able now to go and follow your journey and be part of your story. This networking is powerful, and it is especially well-suited for small businesses and solopreneurs. The individual has such an advantage in 2019 over big companies like Nike and Apple because you have one face and they don't. You can talk to people and be human with them, and this engagement will be the expectation moving forward because it's already starting to happen right now. If you don't have an online brand that's tangible, relevant, relatable, and human, then they will work with the next person that does.

"You might now not be able to spam a 100 people accounts, but you can spend your day searching 10-25 peoples accounts. Consuming their content on all of their social media, looking if they have an Instagram story, what are they into, have they written anything? Go to their podcast and find things that maybe of interest and relevant to them and then humanly introduce yourself and not come off as a robot. To make this work is to approach the interaction as if you want to make a friend," Chelsea said.

For instance, if one person sent Chelsea a message wanting to connect on LinkedIn that sounded like a copied and pasted invitation, she will most likely ignore that advice. The opposite is true if a person reached out to connect and they have a warm introduction and say they enjoyed a podcast she was on, especially minute twenty-three when she brought up social selling for realtors and thanked her for what she had said. Then the person connects with her on a different platform as well, continuing to watch her content and trying to engage in a conversation with her. Then one day, after the person has built up a relationship with Chelsea, they offer her something of value, ranging from content you have created or something you found that pertains to their business or interests. Chelsea will come to them and ask for the services they offer, or they will earn enough street credibility and social to go in for an ask, which will be what you are selling.

"Learning to sell in the context of the current atmosphere is crucial for success in business and marketing."

Individuals Chelsea has coached who apply this tactic are doing it for a year, and they are surprised to find they are spending less and less time prospecting people because their clients are now coming to them. This success is all because people now buy from people, instead of from a business.

CASE STUDY: BOGDAN PADUA

"What is it that we're drawn to? As a community, we're drawn to content, information, and people who make our lives better." Bogdan Padua is a marketing consultant, sales trainer, and cofounder at GetMeMeetings.com, a company dedicated to making it simple and easy to generate sales leads using LinkedIn, email, and phone.

As a dedicated sales person he has learned many skills but the greatest is that you need to flip the mental switch and ask yourself,

> "What can I share that CLEARLY and QUICKLY speaks to what's in it for them and why they should care?" Once you're able to do that effectively and at scale (using social), you'll have reverse engineered the plan that engages your target and grabs their attention.

> Beat obscurity by consistently putting out content that adds value, makes a difference, and inspires community engagement. Master the art of remaining top of mind and you'll have your target audience conditioned to believe your product or service is great, too. You see, most of us are NOT giving our business to the most qualified or the most experienced. Rather, we're going to the first person or organization we think of when we need something. Once you have their attention and you're consistently top of mind, you win. You've heard it before: the more you give, the more you get.

MY STORY OF THE PRINCIPLE:

When I entered into marketing, I was under the impression it would be a cutthroat game, in which the only winners were those who disseminated their information the best. For the most part, I was wrong—a few companies still live with this model, but the vast majority of companies who are excelling do the complete opposite. I have followed this exact principle and seen more benefit than I could ever have imagined. For instance, when it comes to my marketing content, I have shared almost all of the resources that have benefited me. These resources included templates I use, software, how-to videos, and anything else that might bring value to my audience.

By doing this, I have shared a wealth of knowledge with my audience, and intern received numerous clients by doing this exact principle. This strategy works because most information isn't new and is already out there, thus the one that shares it with no expectation of making a sale inevitably gets sales.

ACTION CHECKLIST

Social selling is more about restructuring one's mind-set, but here are a few guidelines to help you understand what to share to enable social media to be a tool that works for you.

- When posting any content, these three points are of upmost importance:

  - A) Providing up-front value

  - B) Being friendly and helpful

  - C) Be yourself

- Much like in physical interactions, get to know the person on the other side of the screen. Ask questions and make it a priority to get to know them on a human level.

- Interact with content to really get to learn about their wants and needs.

- If you think, after consuming their content and establishing a rapport that your offering can benefit them, then take the steps to share it.

"Online hierarchies are inherently dynamic. The moment someone stops adding value to the community, his influence starts to wane."

—GARY HAMEL

"Not adding value is the same as taking it away."

–SETH GODIN

CHAPTER 13

LEAD WITH VALUE

———

"Today it's important to be present, be relevant and add value."

—NICK BESBEAS

"If you get bored with social media, it's because you are trying to get more value than you create."

—FAST COMPANY

IT'S VALUE TIME

Open up your favorite social media app and look at the top people you interact with. Start scrolling through—who do you see? Most of time, they will be friends and family, then a few people you haven't spoken to in a couple of years.

Then, there is someone or a few people that you love to follow. These individuals might be thought leaders in your industry, experts in something you are passionate about, or just someone that you know is an expert on a certain topic. Why do you pay attention to them, consume their content, and interact with them?

Value.

These are the people that provide some sort of value to you— it might be entertainment or might be interesting content, but regardless of what they provide, it's valuable to you. That's why you watch their videos, read their posts, and buy what they offer: they have provided you value.

As humans, we all have this innate desire to give back to our community. This giving back can be in the form of giving money to help the community with a project, supporting a small business down the street, or sharing lessons we have learned through mentorship with others.

Whether through our time or money, we like giving value to others. Have you ever considered giving value even when you have nothing (or it seems as if you have nothing valuable to provide)? For many of us, this can seem like a daunting task, but we seldom realize it could be the exact thing that will help propel us from our current situation into heights once thought unimaginable.

Value is a principle we subconsciously know—we like people who provide value to us—but often don't know how to translate into marketing. That is what Quentin Allums will walk us through today.

I HAD TO BECOME A PERSON OF VALUE

Quentin Allums is the CEO of Urban Misfit Venture, parent company of video and influencer marketing company IEEG and events company MKE Misfits, but above all else, he is a people person. From the outside, it might seem that this young man, one of Wisconsin Inno's "25 Under 25," might have had it easy, but this couldn't be further from the truth.

In high school, Quentin found it challenging to connect and fit in with those around him. He was never quite able to find a community that he felt that he fit right into. This same feeling continued into college.

"In college I would meet so many amazing people, but this time they also found it hard to connect." Unbeknownst to Quentin, they started to gravitate toward him. He had never had the chance to connect with a group in this fashion and saw an opportunity to help create a community for those who also found it hard to connect.[1]

"The community gave me a sense of belonging, but more importantly, it gave me a chance to provide value to people that needed it. I wanted to help those people that don't believe in themselves, that don't have the resources and that don't have the network."

Quentin started to learn that his passion is in helping community members, and providing this value enabled him to build something much bigger than himself.

This feeling of purpose wouldn't leave him even after graduating college in 2016 and taking his first. However, over time, he started to understand that he wasn't providing the value and change he thought he would. He felt a lack of fulfillment and longed for that feeling that he had cultivated while building the community in college.

"I decided to quit my job and take a leap of faith into starting my own company Mad Genie, which focused on providing value and enabling businesses to cultivate their brand, build transactional relationships, and capitalize on overlooked opportunities," Quentin said.

However, in early 2017, after a few months of founding his first company, he had suffered numerous setbacks and had a whopping $900 below $0 in his bank account. Feeling defeated, he gave himself a week to find a client before he would quit and try to get a regular job once again. Through his tireless efforts, leading with value, and a desire to stay true to his mission of providing value, he secured three clients by the end of that week. This low became a blessing in disguise because he saw first hand what could happen when a person sets out to provide value to others, and he would not forget this critical lesson.

FROM ORDINARY TO EXTRAORDINARY

Whether it was in college or business career, he was always pushing the principle of adding value in each situation. He owns one of the fastest growing marketing start-ups in Milwaukee; each of his businesses is focused around the idea of bringing extraordinary value to customers, not only in the businesses he created, but also for the community he built.

He said,

> I started building my misfits community in 2016. It really didn't takeoff until 2018 but I always brought as much value as I could; and brought in people that were smarter than me. I've always said make sure

the community achieves this: everyone needs to feel like they are getting value and providing value. And within that everyone that sees your community from the outside will see that and be more likely to contribute and join your community.

What I discovered was that to have a thriving community you have to focus on first establishing a leader. Once this is done, you have to focus on the 5 or so active members who were always engaged, bring value and showed that they believed in that leader.

"Patience, investment, and clear value prop."

This principle is essential. As new people start to come into the community, they will perceive active engagement as a social norm. These types of communities work because there is an established ecosystem in which everyone gets value. When new people come in, they see that and are much more willing to become involved because they can see that being part of this community brings everyone value.

The value can be as small as simply thoughtfully engaging with other members or making it a point to share opportunities and resources that might be what someone is looking for that you happen to know off. Everyone who sees your community from the outside will see that community engagement and be more likely to contribute and join your community. Quentin also pushes himself to show up as much as he can. Some of him is better than none of him, and so he shows up every day or as much as he can because he aims to create a world and brand so big that everyone has to live in it.

By creating value for your audience, whether as a brand or an individual, people will take notice. They will start to care and have a vested interest in your success.

CASE STUDY: NIKE

Adding value can take many forms, but one company that has especially done a good job is that of Nike. Nike has quickly adapted to changes in technology, having developed their first branded app back in 2006 for the iPod. It has quickly adapted to a host of different apps, such as Nike+ for runners, Nike+ Training Club ,and Nike+ Fuel Lab, which all assist runners and athletes in tracking their progress by setting goals, tailoring workouts and the ability to socially share their efforts with their online community at no cost.[2]

Collectively, these apps boast a user base of over 28 million people. That is 28 million people to which the brand has direct access. With this greater customer intimacy, Nike gains invaluable insights and information about its user base. With access to all this information, Nike could have used it to aggressively drive sales from the app, but instead has brilliantly created a real athlete community by means of its apps. Through this genuine community Nike has built from the ground up, it fosters intense brand loyalty which translates to revenue down the line. (Rose, R. "Want to Prove Content's Success? Stop Measuring It.")

Through this Nike is able to ensure brand loyalty and turn customers into brand ambassadors, which results in a flow of positive reviews and mentions in social media, which helps with brand awareness.

This process is actually mutually beneficial because the user will be getting one of the best mobile apps for strength building at no cost.

MY STORY OF THE PRINCIPLE:

Value is the name of the game in today's marketing world. Getting someone's attention is difficult, but keeping it is equally, if not more, challenging. I have successfully implemented this principle by going into each piece of content with a value-add approach.

I ask myself, "Does this piece of content leave the person consuming it better than before they consumed it?"

If the answer is no, then I don't create or release that content. It's as simple as that.

Once you are known as the value adder, the sky will be the limit. The best example of this occurred when I focused on growing my app company's Instagram account. Before understanding this principle, I would just post aesthetic images with a small caption. Though this wasn't terrible, the pages account stagnated soon after inception. I reviewed why this was and saw the page didn't add any value to the conversation.

It was just pretty to look at.

I decided to do an overhaul and only left pieces that had a pure value add. I started educating my audience about different low-cost adventures, showcasing members of my tribe doing remarkable things in their community, and so on. Though content decreased, engagement skyrocketed because I went in only wanting to add value to the conversation.

ACTION CHECKLIST

- Get a new sheet of paper and write at the top "What is my value proposition?"

  - Then put a line down the page and one side title it "Educate" and the other "Entertain."

- Now brainstorm for five minutes for each of the two sections.

  - It's just brainstorming so feel free to put out any ideas you have

  - For added help, write "My audience would walk away feeling _____ (educated/entertained) because I did _____(answer)

- This checklist will act as your starting block; from now on, circle the top five ideas from the brainstorm session.

- On the back of the page flush out your ideas further.

  - Write four sentences on how you would go about fulfilling each idea

  - Try to cross pollinate each idea with both an entertaining element and educational element.

- Remember, with each piece of content you will learn what is more "valuable" to your audience and be able to better tailor your message as time goes on.

- In the next chapter we will learn more about how to better educate, entertain and engage with your audience

"Try not to become a man of success, but rather try to become a man of value."

—ALBERT EINSTEIN

"Knowledge is of no value unless you put it into practice."

—ANTON CHEKHOV

CHAPTER 14

THE THREE'S

"The key to pursuing excellence is to embrace an organic, long-term learning process, and not to live in a shell of static, safe mediocrity. Usually, growth comes at the expense of previous comfort or safety."

—JOSH WAITZKIN

CONTENT IS KING

So far, we have learned a lot of principles regarding the content creation process, but this next principle directly relates to how to create effective and engaging content. Content works because humans are social creatures. We instinctively gravitate to interacting, socializing, and building relationships with other people. Even in such a digitally connected world, relationships are still one of the most important drivers of success, and that is why we will be shown how to do it effectively from Rachel Pedersen. Rachel has created massive success both in business and social media.

How?

Rachels employs a three-pronged content strategy approach. Having a strong content strategy is one of the best ways you can share your message with the world, and in this chapter, you will learn the best content strategy.

Rachel got her start in the world of marketing when she was still working at one of the top salons in Minneapolis, Minnesota. Rachel dabbled in platforms like Facebook and Twitter but was by far an expert. One day, while at the salon, Rachel learned that one of her client's husband had just purchased a small business and needed a head of marketing. Not one to let an opportunity go, she offered to help and quickly became obsessed with social media marketing

"So I agreed to it, I felt like it was a little bit crazy but our relationship started to grow from there. I became a full time marketing consultant for the company and just moved right into marketing with no degree. I learned everything I possibly could online using Google, Youtube, listening to podcasts

24/7 until I felt like I knew enough about social media to start doing this as a full time gig," Rachel said. [1]

Social media offered Rachel a way to reach customers and an audience that was looking for what she had to offer. She quickly started to see success and realized that this new way of marketing through social media was going to be a game changer for businesses. Though she was learning a lot, she wanted to get more experience, so she decided to apply to market at different media agencies.

It wasn't long before she was able to secure a job at a media agency with a hunger to learn and a little prior experience she had accumulated. While working at this agency, she continued to master and hone her marketing skills. One of the areas that she particularly at which she excelled was creating a successful content strategy that involved digital media such as on Facebook, Instagram, or blogs on websites.

After working and directing marketing at a few different companies, she decided to take on some of her own clients. There reached a point that she was making the same income from her side hustle as she was from her full-time job and had to decide what her next steps would be.

"I decided, you know, I have a few clients, I've got some traction going, I think I could leave my job and become a full-time entrepreneur. So I submitted notice to my job, I gave them one months notice and the very next day I got the email from my biggest client and they said we are terminating our contract, we are bringing all social media in house," Rachel said.

Faced with this obstacle, she re-evaluated her options:

- She could try to reverse the resignation or

- Jump in full force into her company.

In the fall of 2016, she decided to take a leap of faith to do marketing for her clients full-time.

Over the last few years, she has grown both her agency and her online university to new heights by following one central principle: content can be broken down into the principle of the three Es!

The goal of this principle is to create content that allows you to build meaningful relationships with those whom you want to reach. As I have discussed in previous chapters, the new game requires you to focus on building relationships with your audience. All the past principles of finding your niche, understanding your role, and being authentic have led up to this moment.

YOUR CONTENT STRATEGY.

Traditional marketing has been primarily focused on getting a message out to the masses. That was how marketers before the new social reached their audiences. Then everything changed, and today it almost seems foreign to many people to spend time connecting to in order to build meaningful relationships. Most established brands do the opposite because it is much harder to do build relationships than to run advertisements.

Where should you start?

"You need to find the people who are true believers, who are engaging with the content that you are putting out there and do a deep dive into their life," Rachel said. [2]

Taking the time to connect with your audience, customers, and target population will be the key to your growth. Now, learning to create a content strategy enters the picture.

Content will enable you to scale your brand while still retaining the personalized appeal you will need to stand out. These are the three elements that will make up your content strategy:

Engage:

"Engaging with your audience is huge. You see everybody cares most about one person and one person only, I'm sorry to say it, it's not you, it's themselves. Every person cares most about themselves. The more you can engage your audience and ask them questions that have to do with their number one favorite person in the world, the more they are going to engage with it," Rachel said.

Think about your favorite people in the world. When you go out to coffee or dinner with them, they are the ones who ask you questions. They try to get to know you personally and focus on continuing to engage with you often. These are the individuals who don't have an ulterior motive and aren't just connecting to get you over to their house, so they can ask you questions begin their sales pitch.

Educate:

"Education is huge. It's a time where you get to position yourself as an expert, and I don't just mean quoting random facts on social media. What I mean instead is that you focus on teaching your target market things that they normally wouldn't know in a way that intrigues them. Whether its post, quick video or a Facebook live that you put up, go ahead and share something interesting, an insiders secret with your target market. They will thank you for it by giving you organic reach," Rachel said.

This education is not necessarily the traditional school way. Instead, it means to educate individuals by revealing truths, experiences, and sharing a different perspective with those who pay attention to you. You are bringing people into the growth that you are experiencing.

Entertain:

"Entertainment is possibly one of my favorite things to do on social media. It's why I'm super goofy all the time on social media because if we're not having fun. how can the audience? So when it comes to entertainment what you want to do is be the leading source of laughter for your target market, and they're really going to appreciate it. Find a way to create Levity in a topic that's serious or find a way to bring some type of nostalgia that makes people laugh to your industry," Rachel said.

Everyone has different ways to stay entertained. For Rachel, it's humor. Thus, the content she interacts with the most often is the content that make her laugh. She will be much more likely to consume the presented content entirely if it has elements of humor build into it. It is imperative to find out what form of entertainment comes naturally to you and how you go about using it to entertain your audience because ones you can do this effectively and continuously you will get their attention. [3]

REMEMBER YOUR TRAINING

You may have realized that not one of these methods involves direct selling. To build trust, it is imperative not to try and lead with a sales pitch because this will only tarnish the faith you are trying to build with your audience. You want to build such equity with your audience that they come to you to ask for your products.

Rachel very early on made it a point to spend time connecting with her audience, whether as a guest on a podcast or making Skype calls with people she didn't know to answer their questions. Doing these practical activities, though unscalable, helped lay the foundation that would lead to the building of a raving following overtime.

After Rachel was done with a speech to share help with social media, a woman approached her who had been following her content for a while. Without hesitation, she hired Rachel's company on the spot without knowing her exact price for her marketing services. Rachel had no sales pitch because the women felt such a personal connection with Rachel without ever meeting her until that moment.

This process does not happen overnight, nor should it; building meaningful relationships takes time. Even though the process may seem to take a long time, it will eventually propel you to a whole new level of success. You will be focusing on achieving a strong foundation with your audience, which in turn will provide much higher dividends over time. Having a content strategy based on the three Es will open up a window of opportunity for those who are willing to break out of the norm and learn to connect with their audience.

The solution is simple and can be achieved with relative ease once you get the hang of it, which will happen sooner than you expect.

To lay the foundation of building strong relationships, Rachel focused on three Es of content creation which are to engage, educate, and entertain your audience.

MY STORY OF THE PRINCIPLE:

This chapter and conversation with Rachel were equally interesting to me because after the interview, my mind was blown. The three Es made so much sense, and I got started implementing them in my own brand right away. As I have discussed, in the past my content strategy revolved around all three aspects of the relationship funnel in some sort.

Education: I shared tips, tricks, useful resources, my marketing principles, and the ins and outs of how I see marketing though my eyes. This type of content could have been as simple as a how -o video or as complex as an article about your target's mind-set.

Entertain: Each Sunday I continued my #sundayfunday content series, where I would spend time doing a funny dance, sometimes to throwback music, to bring a smile to the faces of my audience members and to have some creative fun.

Engage: I have sent a direct message to 99 percent of the people I have connected to on my social platforms. Sometimes, the message might have been as simple as a thank you, but I take the time and energy to make a real, tangible interaction.

The way I communicate my content, story, and brand is always changing. What has worked in the past few months or weeks may not have the same appeal or reach as it does now. This fluctuation pushes one to experiment. Regardless of what you do with your content strategy, it all can be boiled down to the three E' in the relationship funnel.

ACTION CHECKLIST

- Get a new sheet of paper and separate it into three sections.

- Title each respective section with "Educate," "Entertain," and "Engage."

- Using past notes about your market answer these respective questions:

  - Brainstorm five to ten examples

  - How can I ___(educate/entertain/engage) my target market?

  - What could I put a spin on to __(educate/entertain/engage)?

  - What content that (educate/entertain/engage) do I pay attention to?

  - Who already (educate/entertain/engage) as I want to?

  - How do I like to be (educate/entertain/engage)?

It is important to master these three Es! Make sure to take some time and lay out a strong foundation. For added help, refer to the industry thought leaders and experts to see how they do it. Don't copy them but use them as inspiration.

"Tell me and I forget, teach me and I may remember, involve me and I learn."

—BENJAMIN FRANKLIN

CHAPTER 15

THE SERIES

———

"I Don't Try to Guess What a Million People Will Like. It's Hard Enough to Know What I Like."

—JOHN HUSTON

FIND THE NEEDLE

Think back to the first TV show you fell in love with. You were so obsessed; you would tune in every week just to watch the next episode. Maybe you were obsessed with a movie series like *Harry Potter* or *Star Wars*.

Whether it's TV shows, movies, or online content, we love a good content series. How can you develop a winning content series? This topic is one that Vincent Orleck, a social media veteran and social media manager at ASU knowledge enterprise, has seen in action time and again. Now he will teach us how digital media has the power to transform businesses with a content series, and what needs to be done for you to do the same.

Vincent got his start in marketing back in 2005 when he moved to Phoenix, Arizona, to start a job at one of the at the largest newspaper in the state, The Arizona Republic (also home of azcentral.com), "I was selling ad space for business in both the paper and online."

"However, in 2008/2009, this became difficult because the recession was in full swing and one of the first budget cuts for most companies is always in advertising and/or marketing."

Though this difficulty is understandable, reducing your marketing usually further reduces sales and therefore profitability. Vincent had to find a way to communicate to businesses that they have to continue to market because even with the recession, even with the recession, people still spend money, they're just doing it differently."

He looked for anything that would help bring more revenue to his clients and found a website called Yelp. Yelp is a company that enabled users to generate reviews on companies they have visited. The companies reviewed range from a mechanic shop to hospital to restaurant.

Vincent said,

> My sales territory held quite a few restaurants, so I decided to leverage yelp to convoy to restaurants the importance of continuous branding, marketing and attention to customer service

> I decided to do was physically print out their yelp page with both positive and negative reviews then show businesses what was being said about them. I explained to them that this information was influential for both the potential customers and brand. In turn I established rapport with these businesses and even if people didn't buy from me, it leads to a business relationship.

The more he began to understand platforms like Yelp, the more he became fascinated with digital media and the emergence of social media. A year after implementing this tactic, he decided to take the leap and started to work for Facebook. At the time, Facebook had a pilot program focused on informing any businesses, mainly small and medium-sized businesses, that Facebook offered advertisements. Their small team would also let these businesses know about a free consultation program that Facebook would do if they spend a certain amount of ad money with them.

"I was committed to learning and understanding as much as I could about all avenues of marketing through social media."

The program was centered around helping build ads, understanding how to use their business page, assisting with the ad campaign for that month, and understanding Facebooks analytics. Through this experience, he began to learn what makes a good campaign work and how to create content that kept users coming back for more. Different strategies would need to be done for different clients, but one theme kept emerging that would later be called a content series. This experience showed Vincent the power of social media when used correctly.

After doing this job for a year and seeing the power of digital media, he understood that many businesses didn't harness the full potential of these platforms. Businesses needed to make digital media a priority and learn how to better execute on these new platforms. How are you going to stand out above all the noise?

CREATING LONGEVITY

Today most brands have some social media strategy in their mix of marketing, and they know that they have to be active on social media platforms. What is a common strategy?

The most common strategy is to post a ton of content to as many social platforms as possible. For the last few years or so, businesses big and small have been doing the same things. Thus, advertising has become less active and will continue to get less and less useful unless you find a way to stand out. Why? Most companies follow no theme and are inconsistent. It is almost like throwing darts at a dart board with the lights off. You might hit a bull's-eye, but it is very unlikely.

This strategy has made the Internet so noisy because you are getting bombarded with so much information all the time as a consumer, whether from general informational content or advertisements. How can you avoid this flaw?

Approach content with a plan. You already know your audience, as well as how to create a well-executed content strategy. It's time to make it into a series. (Refer to past chapters if this doesn't ring a bell)

CASE AND POINT

Most companies have a blog, and they use social media in a way to drive people to their website in order to promote the content on their blog post. This strategy has been common for years, and though it might still work, it sure isn't working as well as it was. A new strategy is to create a content series that focuses on giving a reason for a consumer to follow your company on a specific channel.

Take the wildly successful YouTube interview show "Hot Ones," a series of videos that involve celebrities being interviewed while eating increasingly spicy chicken wings. This show is produced by the magazine *Complex,* which focuses on trends in style, pop culture, music, sports, and sneakers with a focus on street wear, sneaker culture, hip-hop, and graphic art. The magazine stands out from the crowd by being different, entertaining, and providing value in a unique setting that people want to watch. This identity, in turn, enhances the brand and gives people an incentive to pay attention to the company, leading to additional revenue.

Content series enable you to maintain a general theme behind your content, create consistency, and start to cultivate a strong following that has incentive to return. Your goal is to create a series that incorporates the three Es in a unique way.

Some examples of successful content series include:

- "#askgaryvee" by Gary Vaynerchuck

- "Impact Theory" by Tom Bilyeu

- "The Therapist" by VICE

How can you create a content series for your brand? It depends on your brand's message, its authentic image, and your niche. Making the series will involve creativity and the checklist below will help you brainstorm.

WHATS THE RESEARCH SAY

Researchers conducted a case study to demonstrate the effectiveness of having a content series collaboration titled "Science and *Star Wars* with IBM." This ten-part series kicked off in fall 2017 primarily on Facebook, because "the *Star Wars* universe is filled with unbelievable technology, but a glance into IBM Research's labs and Watson's services reveals we may be closer than we think. With *Star Wars* and IBM, science fantasy meets science reality."

The strategic partnership turned out to be a success, with an estimated 1,123,238 views on YouTube and 13,509,958 on Facebook. The ten episodes were able to reach an estimated 14,633,196 views while simultaneously giving exposure to new audiences for both IBM and *Star Wars*. In exploring interesting topics such as light savers and helper robots, the videos were entertaining and concise, with an average episode length of five minutes long.

The series would go on to become a finalist to be a branded series on Facebook because "Science and *Star Wars* successfully integrated Watson, along with IBM researchers and scientists, to showcase IBM's technological achievements. The campaign also successfully leveraged fans of *Star Wars* and showed them IBM's abilities within the tech realm. Through the 'Science and *Star Wars*' videos, IBM was able to connect in new ways with *Star Wars* fans while still reaching their intended demographics of developers, IT decision makers, and technology professionals."

MY STORY THE PRINCIPLE:

Serialized content creates audience investment and gives them an incentive to "stay tuned to the next episode." I have seen these types of series work wonders for me, especially for Instagram and LinkedIn. On each of these platforms, I identified a topic of interest to my audience and worked backwards to develop a series that would serve those interests. For example, on LinkedIn I tried to find a way to share marketing content and discovered on #MarketingMonday.

Each Monday I created a short video about tips and tricks to succeeding in digital media. I created a unique introduction and layout to differentiate my content from that of competitors. My series gathered a loyal following of community members who expected an educational video in the #MarketingMonday series each week.

- Regularly focus on the needs of your audience across the sales funnel.

- Build expectations for what content your audience can come to expect.

- Establish your business as a subject matter expert through repetition.

- Engage with customers, providing them ongoing value in addition to your offerings.

- Provide answers to your customers' problems through storytelling.

ACTION CHECKLIST

- For a content series, get a sheet of paper and title the page content series on top.

- Next, list out five topics that are related to your brand.

  - These topics should include items that you think can provide value to your audience.

  - Spend five minutes brainstorming.

  - You want to focus on what resources you have available and the way that you think you can create content that will bring people back.

  - There is no need to reinvent the wheel; think of series that you already love and borrow the concepts from them.

- Series are simply defined as a set of related information around a key topic in which each piece is a digestible chunk of information that can stand on its own but ties into a centralized topic at the end.

  - After you've finished brainstorming, search your idea on Google to get inspiration for each idea.

    - If you are still having trouble, consider why you watch the talk shows you watch online, why you listen to your podcasts, or why you consume any content regularly.

- Keep digging into why you gravitate to that

- Pick one that seems the most feasible and that you think can bring the most value to your audience.

- Remember to have fun with this process; much like your favorite TV show, you want to make this fun and enjoyable. The series doesn't have to involve a massive infusion of resources. Test your ideas and aim for the lowest hanging fruits.

"We tend to do period stuff because it helps make it one step removed from boring everyday reality."

—ETHAN COEN

CHAPTER 16

EXPERIMENT

"Observation is a passive science, experimentation an active science."

—CLAUDE BERNARD

"All life is an experiment. The more experiments you make the better."

—RALPH WALDO EMERSON

DEFINE IT

Do you remember the first time you got behind a wheel of a car? It was a scary experience—nothing you had ever done before even remotely resembled the experience. You had no experiences or past skills to pull from, but you tried it. The more you practiced and experimented, the better you become.

You didn't get it on the first try because it wasn't natural. Slowly, you started to get better, and with each passing session, you grew more confident.

Why? Because you had a chance to experiment.

Some of the best lessons you have ever learned, such as driving a car, came through experimentation. These experiments that might have yielded a success or failure at the moment, but, regardless, they were pivotal events that taught you something.

Marketing is no different.

The platforms, tips, tricks, and best practices are always changing, in part due to fluctuation in customer interests, but also because of your competition. If a competitor sees something that is working, they will try to replicate it; if it works for you, then surely it must work for them. As more marketers replicate you, that special way of communicating with the customer becomes standard practice. Once it's standard practice, then customers no longer feel you are that unique.

You have to be constantly trying new things, whether that be how you present your message, or on what platforms you market. With the help of Mark Metry, you will learn that experimenting is a requirement of today's marketer.

Mark Metry, host of Humans 2.0 podcast, one of the Top 100 in the world, and founder of VU dream, a virtual reality company, is no stranger to experimenting. Mark has seen firsthand how crucial it is to constantly be experimenting and has based his career on pushing the boundaries of whatever he does. In this chapter, we will learn exactly how to build experimentation into our routine and leverage it to our advantage.

"EXPERIMENTS ARE NOT JUST LIMITED TO DRIVING OR CHEMISTRY CLASS"

When Mark was fifteen years old, he became obsessed, like many other kids his age, with Minecraft. He loved the simplicity of the game and enjoyed being immersed in the game's culture. It wasn't long before he noticed a few improvements that could be made to enhance the experience. The more he played, the more he began to imagine how much better it would be if someone could just implement these changes.

When the changes didn't happen, a wild idea popped into his mind: he should start his own Minecraft community and server himself.

Mark said,

> I did this just for fun, and with no marketing or business experience I set out to build this community.
>
> I didn't expect this to grow as much as it did. All I wanted was to create something I wanted. In the early days we experimented a lot because we could and wanted to, I mean we were building this thing from scratch. Slowly more and more people started to join and before I knew it I had a company on my hands.

With no marketing experience, he set out to try an assortment of tactics and strategies, many of which didn't yield results. Though he didn't have a playbook for success, he knew that with effort and experimenting he could figure it out. He kept pushing, and finally had a major breakthrough with mastering SEO (search engine optimization). SEO worked by optimizing your website to get organic traffic from the search engine results page such as Google.

Through many tests, he managed to rank as one of the top search results for keywords that his niche was looking for. He was then able to scale much more quickly and effectively, so he decided to double down on it. At its peak, the network that Mark had created boasted over ten million users and a remote staff of over forty employees.

Mark, at a very young age, had built a company and learned to market it, all from a thought and an experiment.

"THE NEXT FRONTIER"

Though Mark was happy with what he built, but he was hungry for something new. After marketing the server for a few years, Mark began to see the progressive rise of influence that social media was bringing to the playing field.

"As I grew up and became more entrenched in social media, I began to see a trend with people becoming thought leaders, influencers and those who had created a great brand by leveraging social," he said.

He didn't know exactly how, but Mark recognized that new power dynamics lay in this concept. Much like his previous experiences, he jumped in and experimented to build his own brand online. He first started to study what makes these people so successful.

Mark spent hours testing and experimenting with different media and avenues, but with little success. He turned to some experts he thought would help him. To get more information on brand, Mark interviewed Quentin Allums, mentioned in the chapter about value, for his "Humans 2.0" podcast.

"I wanted to understand where to start and what better way to find that out than asking someone who has been in my shoes."

Quentin emphasized that Mark had to triple down on creating content, every day, on LinkedIn especially. This strategy had worked for Quentin and made him one of the top influencers on the platform. Mark's mind was blown, and he changed his perception of creating his brand. Mark's strategy until this interview was to share more of others' content than his own, but, after listening to Quentin, he decided the people following him were there to follow him, and he had to create more content for them.

"As you are taking action your going to fail a lot. You are going to fall, make mistakes and mess up. But the fact of the matter is if you consistently show up, you have the opportunity to take in one of the most data rich information systems out there which is failure. It's as simple as that. Just show up again and again."

Mark used tips like these as a reference point and as the basis of his content strategy moving forward. After seeing the success of others who had used this formula, he decided he would try exactly to emulate them. His mission became clear to him.

"I wanted to establish myself as a thought leader in the VR space and knew I had to be different to stand out and get attention. Every day I would create content that either was a personal/emotion or shared knowledge and expertise in what I was doing."

His content included sixty-second videos on LinkedIn or Instagram, pictures, quotes, texts, and articles. Constant experimentation with different types of content, styles, and a host of other mechanisms gave him a clearer understanding of what worked for him and his audience. Mark focused on being authentic and honest with his audience while sharing his experiences as an entrepreneur in the VR.

After showing up and posting every day, trust started to be established between him and his audience.

"I was testing out a lot with my video content. Out of nowhere my following started to steadily increase and I began to become more well known in the LinkedIn community," Mark said.

Mark found his voice. Through constant experimentation, he found what worked for him, and his engagement began to reflect it. To this day, Mark continues to experiment with new types of content, platforms, and styles.

As of the writing of this chapter in April 2019, Mark has made an announcement in a recent episode of his podcast that he will be trying out a new question on his show.

"On the 'Humans 2.0' podcast, I started experimenting with an ending element to the show to give the audience a more actionable thought or tool to utilize in life. I ask all of my extremely successful and impactful guests to leave the audience with a self-inquisitive question that you can ask yourself throughout the day and really ponder." [1]

Even small experiments such as the one above help him to stay up to date with changes, including new algorithms on each social platform or more compelling ways to connect meaningfully with his audience. Once Mark got into this experimentation, he noticed there was much less competition that he thought. When he started his podcast, he was scared that few, if any, people would listen to it. A year in, his podcast was ranked one of the Top 100 podcasts in the world because he showed up and put in the effort to create content for his audience.

CASE STUDY: L'ORÉAL

One company that has focused on continuous experiential marketing is L'Oréal. The cosmetic company was founded in 1909 and has become one of the largest companies in its industry. The company's culture has really embraced testing and experimenting as a core part of its business.

In an interview, Nadine McHugh, senior vice president of omni media strategy, strategic investments, and creative solutions for L'Oréal USA, explains, "For us, it's always about what's next. We're proud of our past, but we want to maintain our leadership in the beauty industry, and that means testing, co-creating and innovating with our media partners on a regular basis." One example of this experimental attitude was back in 2016 when the company launched the campaign "Essie's Naming Department."[2]

The campaign focused on experimenting with YouTube stars and digital agencies to develop a video series aimed at communities the company had yet to reach. The company felt there was a lot of synergy among these groups, and L'Oréal wanted to showcase that in a different way. From this campaign, the company has reached an estimated 3.5 million views from Facebook and YouTube. Even if this experiment isn't a home run, the company can still gain from it in a number of ways. The company has a built-in "learning agenda."

That's where we outline what questions we're looking to answer, what new insights we'd like to uncover, and the steps that we'll take to get there.

MY STORY OF THE PRINCIPLE:

In a world filled with so much content, I have seen people who demonstrate a continuous value add to their content win. When I deconstructed the strategy of the people I follow, nearly all the people had some type of personal narrative in their content.

I noticed that the people to whom I feel most connected were the ones that have shared their failures as well as their successes with their audience, creating a sense of vulnerability. I feel as though I can trust them more. I thought, "OK, I have never posted about any of my failures before; maybe I should try it."

For instance, I was hesitant to create videos about my lack of marketing knowledge before I came into the industry. I felt as if people knew that I didn't get a degree in marketing, that I must be less qualified than others. I just didn't see the benefit— I thought I must have been the only one who had gone through these mistakes, such as not knowing what a KPI (key performance index) was in a client meeting.

I realized that in sharing those failures, I was sharing stories and lessons that would help someone not make the same mistakes. I was creating value, and I didn't know if this tactic would resonate with my audience because I had never even tried it.

I made a video detailing my fear and insecurities about my marketing background and posted it online. To date, these videos are the most viewed and most engaging pieces of content I have created. I would have never known the power of sharing my mistakes unless I took the leap and experimented.

ACTION CHECKLIST

- On a new sheet of paper, title this section "Experiment."

- Then spend ten minutes writing down all the marketing tactics your brand or company has yet to implement.

  - Do not limit yourself—go as crazy as you want, but make sure you write it all down.

- Now, pick a few and see if any direct competitors— ones in your industry—and indirect competitors—ones who vie for the same solution—have implemented any of the above tactics.

- Learn about the opportunities and pitfalls that might come with these tactics.

- Now, armed with this research, ask yourself if there is a low– or no cost way to implement your favorite ideas as experiments

  - Cost is not just limited to capital, but also includes time and additional resources.

- Test your strategy a few times to give you enough data to see if it is effective.

"A fool is a man who never tried an experiment in his life."

—ERASMUS DARWIN

"How could youths better learn to live than by at once trying the experiment of living?"

—HENRY DAVID THOREAU

CHAPTER 17

RESOURCEFULNESS

"Life's too short to hang out with people who aren't resourceful."

—JEFF BEZOS

"A resourceful person will always make a opportunity fit his or her needs."

—NAPOLEON HILL

RESOURCEFULNESS OVER RESOURCES

Tony Robbins once said, "Success is not about your resources. It's about how resourceful you are with what you have!" For you who are just getting started in the marketing world, you might feel intimidated by the lack of resources at your disposal.

It could be that you don't have the most excellent camera, a handsome sum of marketing dollars, or even a full-stack marketing team, but none of that should stop you. With the Internet reaching maturity, the world is in the palm of your hand—you need to learn to be resourceful. Justin Nguyen, marketing consultant, co-host of the "Young and D.U.M.B." (dedicated, up and coming, motivated and bold) podcast, has mastered.

"WHAT DO I HAVE"

We all start life with different resources—some have more, some have fewer. I have learned and seen firsthand that even with a lack of resources, you can still rise to the top of your industry and make a difference. Justin further demonstrated this principle.

Justin embodied the spirit of resourcefulness even before the podcast, and his personal brand was the start. In college, he would continually strive for a 4.0 GPA while squeezing in study time and late-night networking events, all to meet the people who would help propel him into whichever field he wanted. When the idea for the podcast was conceived, Justin turned to his best friend, Gary Pershad. Gary and Justin had been friends for a while but had gone to different colleges.

Neither one of the guys knew anything about setting up and running podcasting, so they dedicated the whole summer break to learning as much as they could about the podcast space. "We decided just to jump in, learn but with the goal to get a few episodes recorded."

"To get started it was just Google. Google, Google, Google and one of the first reoccurring things that came up was that you need to produce that first episode. No matter how bad it's gonna be," Justin said. [1]

Their first mission was to purchase the cheapest microphone that they could find, and they finally found one for $50. After that, they secured their first interviewee and recorded soon after that. Because they didn't have money for more microphones, they had to sit around a table and move the mic back and forth whenever someone spoke. Though the audio wasn't the best, they made it work, and a few months later decided to upgrade and get another one. Fall soon approached, and each host went back to his respective school, but this separation did not slow down the podcast, and as time passed the team started to secure more prominent names for the podcast.

They did this by leveraging the attention that Instagram had. What Justin, and especially his Chief Communication Officer Michelle Bultmann did, was utilize this platform to find and connect business development with people they think could be potential guests on the podcast.

Once a person of interest has been identified, they contact that person through direct message. If the person does not respond, further investigation is necessary to find that person again through Instagram. Most of the time, most accounts they look at have email addresses in the bios. From this strategy, they have had a diverse and influential stream of interviews that has further grown their podcast.

"Resourcefulness is making do what's given to you. Whether you have a lot of a little, it all depends on how you use it. And I think the beauty of social media is that there is no barrier. You just can't be scared of the mindset of being scared holds so many people back."

PATIENCE AND PERSISTENCE

The "Young and D.U.M.B." podcast has been going for over a year now and each episode gets hundreds of downloads. Even if they don't get as many downloads as others, they continue to put out content twice a week. The team knows that success and thousands of listeners won't come overnight but remain patient as they see the steady increase. As much as numbers do matter, the team focuses on their impact and using their resources to bring value to their audience. Justin, for example, has further used the podcast to amass a sizeable following on LinkedIn that has provided him with countless opportunities and the ability to connect with more people.

After graduating from college in December 2018, Justin decided to pursue his company and podcast full-time. Though he doesn't have a marketing degree, he decided to dedicate as much time as he could to understanding the industry. He started to dedicate time to interviewing marketers, much like I did, to learn what made them successful. He began to read the books, the "marketing classics" as he put it. He began to practice and move what he was learning from theory into practical use cases. He never let the lake of resources that he had to limit him.

"Resourcefulness is making do what's given to you. Whether you have a lot of a little, it all depends on how you use it."

Justin has taught me that regardless of the situation you are in, there is always a way to use what you have to your advantage.

WHATS THE RESEARCH SAY

The more resourceful you are, the more creative you will be at solving your problems or achieving your goal. A perfect example of this is Sophia Christina Amoruso, who founded Nasty Gal, a women's fashion retailer. Sophia had no marketing budget, but she did have a knack to just listen to her customers and tweak accordingly. [2]

> Back then, she selected her best shots for eBay and posted them on MySpace to get a more qualitative feel. If the bids were lower than she expected and the comments on MySpace were negative, she'd ditch the model and sell the same item on someone new. Now, she still can't stop meddling. When a wrap dress was getting just one sale a week, she insisted it is put on a popular model. The dress became a top seller at 400 buys a week.

> "I just tried to elevate everything, whether it was exciting or not. eBay taught me a lot about perceived value, and how to make things look their best. We didn't really spend any money on marketing. The whole time we've just listened and tweaked, listened and tweaked, and listened and tweaked, and that's what we're still doing.... It's what's great about online." (Barret, V. "Nasty Gal's Sophia Amoruso: Fashion's New Phenom.")

By June of 2012, the company had earned $128 million in sales, with gross margins of more than 60 percent.

MY STORY OF THE PRINCIPLE

When I entered this world of marketing, I didn't have a formal degree. I didn't have any background in marketing, but I knew I had dedication. As most of what I do in marketing has to do with lack of resources, I want to share seedling that sparked it all. What I needed to do was start at square one. I accumulated every marketing book I could get my hands on; I listened to every marketing podcast I could find. I began to build a foundation, laying each brick one at a time.

After I had a sound foundation, I decided to start working for free at start-ups, helping with whatever I could in their marketing departments. I would do the most seemingly mundane tasks, but to me, they were all new. I went from company to company, finding anyone who was willing to teach me anything about marketing. I started to amass a skill set, began to learn from their experiences and, slowly but surely, start to see myself as a marketer. The next phase was the hardest.

The next step was to become a real practitioner of all the skills I had accumulated. I applied it to a small app start-up I had started, PakPak. Then I landed a job as a growth hacker, a.k.a. a marketer at a start-up. Through hours of time, investment, and the willingness to use whatever resources I got my hands on, I transformed myself into the marketer you see today. I am far from where I want to be, but I am closer today than I was yesterday. Don't let the lack of resources stop you, your brand, or your company.

ACTION CHECKLIST

The point of this chapter was to illustrate that you don't need all the resources in the world to be a success, but instead, you need to be resourceful with what you have. Justin and Michelle used the Internet to both land guests and learn about podcasting.

- Get a new piece of paper and list resources at the top.

- Divide the sheet into three sections: "Resources I currently have"/ "Resources I can get"/ "Dream resources"

- Next, list out as many resources as you can for each.

- Then fill out these three sections:

  - Resources I currently have

    - What resources do I currently have on hand to help me reach my goal?

    - Are these resources adequate, or will I need additional resources? If so what are they?

- How can I best utilize the resources I have to help me achieve my goals?

   - Resources I can get

- What additional resources must I acquire?

- How will I acquire these resources?

- Have I Googled other resources that are to me? If not, do so.

   - Dream resources

- Is this dream resource really that out of reach?

- Is there someone or some organization that I know that can get me closer to this resource?

- Is there something that I currently have that I could barter to get this resource (product, service, time, money)?

"If you're the type of person who has to fulfill your dreams, you've gotta be resourceful to make sure you can do it."

—VIN DIESEL

CHAPTER 18

CUSTOMER SERVICE

———

"People do not care how much you know until they know how much you care."

—TEDDY ROOSEVELT

"Customer service should not be a department. It should be the entire company."

—TONY HSIEH

"PLEASE COMPLAIN AWAY"

Up until this point, we have talked extensively about the principles of success within the new framework of marketing. How does customer service fit into this?

On the surface it might not, but if you look a little deeper, you will see that marketing comprises a range of specific activities, all of which aim to promote your products, services, or brands. Customer service is a way that you are able to showcase your brand's story, message, and values in a personalized manner.

Yet we dread reaching out to most companies customer service departments.

Why?

Few companies make customer service a priority, and that's where the advantage for you lies. If you are able to impact a customer in a positive way through a well-executed customer service intervention, you leave a long-lasting impression on the customers—one that will not only create word of mouth marketing for you, but will also get you raving fans of your brand.

I am going to jump into how to do customer service right with Jay Baer, author, speaker, and founder of Convince & Convert Consulting, a digital marketing and customer experience advisory firm that helps the world's most iconic brands gain and keep more customers.

IT'S ALL ABOUT THE CUSTOMER

Jay Baer was born in Lincoln, Nebraska, but grew up in Lake Havasu City, Arizona. After attending the University of Arizona and receiving his degree in political science, he spent numerous years in politics—definitely not the most comfortable place for anyone dealing with customer service. In 2000, John McCain was running for office, and Jay was put in charge of his direct mail program and creation of his website.

"I saw first hand how it was possible for someone to leverage the Internet for marketing purposes and was hooked. I knew I had to learn more about how technology was going to impact media and set forth to master digital media marketing," Jay said. [1]

Later in 2000, he started his first digital agency, Mighty Interactive. The company specialized in email marketing and online advertising solutions for numerous corporate clients. Understandably, Jay was able to be utterly entrenched in the digital media landscape and slowly mastered his craft as a practitioner. After a merger in 2008, he moved on to create a social media strategy consulting company called Convince & Convert. Over the last few years, after building and working with numerous organizations, Jay saw a new opportunity that many brands had ignored: customers complaints.

"People who complained were not the problem; it was the fact that brands were ignoring them."

Moving forward, if you and your brand want to "win" at customer service, you have to stop ignoring customer complaints and start to fix them.

How?

"What that means in practice, operationally, that you answer every customer, in every channel, every time. Instead of what we actually do today which is to answer some customers, that our boss prefers, when we get around to it and we aren't doing something else," Jay said.

It is no longer acceptable to ignore the feedback and complaints of your customers. We have been programmed to see complaints as negative, rather than see them as an opportunity. Thus, we tend to push them off to the very last second and say we will get to them when we get to them. What if we never respond to them?

How would you feel in this situation?

"No response is a response. No response is a response that says we don't care about you or your opinions whatsoever."

You would be upset and now will be more agitated than ever because humans don't like to feel ignored, especially by brands they trusted with their hard-earned money. This cycle of not listening and responding to your customers will only lead to more significant trouble down the road. Excellent customer service makes sense because it is one of the best ways to keep existing customers, which is more cost-effective—retaining customers is much less expensive than having to replace them.

MAKE THIS PRACTICAL

Take as an example a person who is an influencer in the fashion space with fifty thousand followers on Instagram. Let's say she purchases a pair of yoga pants, but she is unsatisfied with the quality of some she receives. She reaches out to the company multiple times, but each time hears nothing. In frustration, she posts a video and expresses her concerns about the leggings. Thousands of spectators watch as the brand ignores this negative, publicly broadcast message from a customer.

This example shows how a brand can take a lousy situation and make it worse; now she is not just upset about the quality of the leggings, but she is also ignored. No response is a response because it communicates to your customers is you don't care about them or their response at all. Those customers who complain should be viewed as the most important customers, as they represent those people who are willing to voice how they genuinely feel about the experience of the brand.

What would have happened if that brand had stepped up, addressed her concerns, and fixed the problem the first time? How much more likely would that influencer have been to not just speak more highly of the brand, but also publicly talk about her fantastic experience with her large audience?

It is imperative to view customers as a subset of a much larger group because not all customers who are dissatisfied complain. The more you can address complaints about a wide range of topics, the better you will understand the pain points of your customer and be able to improve them accordingly.

"When you answer a customer complaint, not necessarily solve it, just say we hear you it increases customer advocacy and customer loyalty. And both of those effects happen across all customer contact mechanisms: phone, email, social media, review sites, discussion boards and forms. It's if you answer they like you better if you don't answer they like you less," Jay said.

BREAK IT DOWN

So where should you start?

"Actively seek out complaints because when you receive compliments, even if it makes you feel terrific, you seldom learn anything."

Most of the time we already know we are good at, and absorbing excessive compliments has the potential to blind a person from reality. One hidden benefit is that when customers complain, relevant content can be generated around answering that question. Again, if one customer has a complaint or problem, odds are they are not alone. Therefore, as you identify more questions and concerns, you can generate more relevant content for your customers.

"Out of every 100 dissatisfied customers, five actually complain in a way that you can find it. So what this means is those people who actually take the time to tell you that you're less than perfect are representatives of a much alleger group of dissatisfaction," Jay said.

Though it may seem counterintuitive, you should strive to get more complaints from your customers. Jay gives the example of a bakery, where, as part of a new initiative, the company looked at tripling their complaints because they understood that with each complaint, there was an opportunity to learn something about our customers.

The bakery understood this information would help them build and change processes that would over time increase their customers' satisfaction and decrease complaints. They sought to understand all points of contact that they had with their customers, such as email, video, and in-store experiences, and kindly added a nudge for feedback. By expressing to your customers your desire for feedback and complaints, you will not just learn different ways to serve them better, but also publicly make a statement that you listen to your customers, and that is where the real advantage lies.

Listening to your customers has the potential to create meaningful content and better improve their perception of your brand. Improvement starts by making customer service a priority and responding to every single complaint, every single time, on every platform.

"Customer service is the new marketing. Everything else about your business can and will be stolen by your competitors. They will copy your products. They will copy your price, they will copy your marketing, they will copy your social media marketing. The one thing that they cannot copy from you, the one thing they cannot steal from you is whether or not you fundamentally care more about your customers than they do. it's not sealable; it's not copyable; that's your competitive advantage," Jay said.

CASE STUDY: SOUTHWEST AIRLINES

Southwest Airlines is a perfect example of the power of customer service. "Customer service was not just a mantra nor was it a flavor of the week. It was a mindset established from the birth of the company; a living, breathing philosophy that manifested itself in all facets of our business." [2]

The carrier that caters to more than 100 million passengers annually lists customer service as its core mission: The mission of Southwest Airlines is dedication to the highest quality of Customer Service delivered with a sense of warmth, friendliness, individual pride, and Company Spirit. The dedication to service is working, as Southwest Airlines has bucked industry trends by delivering 42 consecutive years of profitability.

Southwest Airlines has adapted their use of social media as a way to scale its reach. "The Marketing team as Southwest maintains a single Twitter handle for both marketing and [customer] service. We wanted everything to mirror our brand and voice, whether it's a customer service interaction or a marketing post." If you really break down the model,

"Southwest has created a 'recipe of how we engage with our customers,' which includes four key steps:

1. Welcoming the customer,

2. Finding out what their problem is,

3. Researching their problem, and

4. Giving them a resolution.

"Our customers, they're in the moment dealing with the situation, so they want an answer as soon as possible," he says, adding that Southwest's goal is a ten-to-fifteen-minute response time.

"Don't forget that the customer is at the middle of the model, and what it is that they want in an experience is what we should be providing and delivering. A lot of times we get in our four walls of our offices, and we build what we think they want, or what we think would be cool, and that's not exactly the right formula for success." [3]

MY STORY OF THE PRINCIPLE:

My first job ever was in retail, and my time there showed me firsthand how excellent customer service can impact an experience. It is often in these situations that you can turn an upset customer into a raving fan, or vice versa The best digital media situation happened when I first started marketing for PakPak. We established our social media pages and were a few weeks into building up the community. We began by showcasing some of our community members.

We were seeing massive local engagement but while posting one of our member's pictures, I forgot to tag her in it. A week later I got a distressed message from this community member, expressing her frustrations about the situation.

I decided to listen to what she had to say and try not to get offended at what she was saying, which was my first reaction. After just a few minutes I understood that she wasn't upset with me necessarily—it was just a miscommunication, and I was able to resolve it on the spot. Today, she is one of our most supportive community members all because I took the time to understand and fix the problem.

ACTION CHECKLIST

- Get a new piece of paper or word document and title the page "Customer Service."

  - At this point, we know a lot about where our customer's attention is focused. but now it's time for us to learn what we can do better.

- Spent thirty minutes browsing the Internet to search for your business or organization reviews.

  - Popular sites include: Apart from the usual social media accounts such as Facebook, leverage other sites such as Yelp, Reddit, and Angie's List

  - If these yield little results, use Google to search for "(Your company/organization) reviews."

- Write out all negative complaints.

  - Remember, the more you have, the better.

- Once you have sufficient complaints, highlight common problems.

  - These must be addressed first.

- Each complaint will be different and unique to the industry but make it a priority to fix them. I know it can be hard; trust me. In the end, it will pay off!

For further steps:

  - Make it part of your marketing strategy to answer complaints on your social pages.

- Find ways, just like the bakery above, to triple your complaints and push customers for honest feedback. The more you know, the better and faster you can address the problems, which will leave you with happier customers and a better brand.

"Excellent customer service is the number one job in any company! It is the personality of the company and the reason customers come back. Without customers, there is no company!"

—CONNIE ELDER

CHAPTER 19

TIME

"Yesterday is gone. Tomorrow has not yet come. We have only today. Let us begin."

—MOTHER THERESA

OUR MOST FINITE RESOURCE IS TIME

Let's be honest, we all feel there is not enough time in the day! If I could offer you anything in the world, more time would definitely be at the top of that list, wouldn't it?

We don't get time back; as a marketer, you will never have all the time you want. In this chapter, we will learn about the importance of proper time management and how to maximize this resource to your advantage.

When I cofounded PakPak, I was a full-time student, had a part-time job, and had a bustling social life. When I decided to join the team, my first priority was to learn how to invest little time into this project but produce massive results. What was the magical formula?

There wasn't one.

There was no way to spend a few hours a week as a marketer, especially because, at the time, I didn't even know marketing. Through many failures, tactics, and lessons, I did start to learn a thing or two about how to market more effectively.

That being said, you will have to invest time into marketing! There's no way around that, but I can assure you, the more you invest, the better the outcome will be. Even if you don't see success right away, you are building a foundation that will be strong and ready for your next initiative.

BUCKETS

In 2018, I started to "market." I have market in quotation marks because, at that time, I had no idea what I was doing. I was posting pretty pictures on Facebook and Instagram. I wasn't telling stories, finding my niche, or providing any value. As you can imagine, doing this week after week I started to get frustrated with my page's growth. I was posting every day—why wasn't my brand's exploding?

The answer: I wasn't putting in the time.

That's right—was spending five minutes every day, so why wasn't I seeing results?

It takes time to make anything significant, not just because you are patient, but because time is the one resource you have at your disposal. I didn't have money for a marketing team, but I had time; I didn't have influencer friends to promote my pages, but I had time; I didn't have any working knowledge of how to run an ad, but I had time.

And so do you.

How do you spend your time wisely for maximum effect? By using buckets.

Buckets are nothing more than place holders of your time. They are a simple way to gauge how much time to invest in different parts of your marketing strategy. The bucket approach is quite similar to Rachel Pederson's three Es principle but is adapted for the wider strategy you have at hand. The bucket approach focuses on putting together many small tasks into one block of time and completing those tasks at a specific time. Whether writing, designing, or responding to direct messages, there's a certain momentum we get when working on certain tasks for an extended period of time.

Simply put, we are using Newton's First Law of Motion: "An object in motion, stays in motion."

I decided I wanted to get serious about marketing; that being said, I still had limited time and that is where bucketing came to be so important. Through many tests, I have developed my own strategies to scale my efforts and use my time effectively. I have learned to break my marketing efforts into daily batches by scheduling time off to do each bucket. Below is my schedule, but test what works best for your needs, time restraints, and outcomes.

Here are all the buckets I have used as a marketer, all based on the idea of time batching.

Messages

Most places we market use some form of built-in direct messaging system. This feature is a fantastic tool to use because it enables you to send messages directly customer, client, or potential ally. You have the potential to grow a meaningful relationship, one that could lead to a business partnership, new customer, or referral. However, most marketers do not use this tool because it can be time intensive. I have created templates below that will help you streamline your messaging efforts. I recommend batching time and sending a message to all followers or connections. The response rate may vary, but the return on investment potential far exceeds the time you spend.

Thank you/ Response messages template:

Hi (name of person, organization, company) ✳ (use a brightly colored emoji to grab readers attention),

I hope you are having a fantastic (day of week or time of day)! I just wanted to say thank you for (engagement on a piece of content, website visit or whatever that person did to inspire you to write to them).

(Remind them about that piece of content or passion you have for the product/service/industry).

Thank you again.

Have such a good day! (give them one more piece of kindness)

Introduction messages template:

Hi (name of person, organization, company) ✳ (Use a brightly colored emoji to grab readers attention),

Just wanted to send a quick message. It's so awesome (if awesome is not in your vocabulary use another word to convey excitement) to e-meet you!

(Discuss your passion/occupation/ interests, want to develop report with this new connection)

Example: Please let me know if I can ever bring any value to you! I love sharing my knowledge especially in regards to marketing or branding! Anyway, it is so amazing to have connected!

(Optional: ask an open-ended question to solicit a potential response)

Have a great day 🌷 (give them one more piece of kindness})

Community engagement

Community engagement refers to responding to comments on content. A comment is one of the easiest ways for community members to engage with your content. Likes tend are more passive, but a comment is a much more active interaction. It is important to section off time to respond to these comments because if you spend a set amount of time of responding, then you will be able to more effectively complete the task in less time.

Much like with messages, if you spend time replying to each comment, you have a much higher chance of building a real relationship with that person. Taking initiative sets you apart from your competition because most brands do not focus on responding. Responding to comments is a practical, low-cost way to add a personal touch to your marketing efforts.

Content full stack (creation and editing)

The content bucket is equally important. Creating any type of content can be time and effort intensive. That being said, I do recommend picking two to three times a week to dedicate to content creation. Creating content, especially meaningful and valuable content, takes time. Setting up content creation in this framework will enable you to more effectively create content.

The same goes for editing your creation. Whether you are proofreading an article, adding captions to a video, or stitching together a podcast, you need to section off time to do that. I recommend you find one or two days—some content will require less time and some more, but sitting down on

Tuesday to edit blogs and Friday to edit videos will help you complete these tasks.

Outreach

Outreach is another outstanding opportunity to reach and market to our target audience. It can take the form of a direct message or a comment. You want to first identify why it is you are reaching out—is it to gain a potential audience member, fan, or collaboration, or just to network with someone in your industry?

For outreach template messages:

Hey (name of person, organization, company) ⚡ (use a brightly colored emoji to grab the readers attention),

You keep popping as a Suggested Connection. I see in your profile (mention something that you saw in their title, past content or something to build rapport with that individual.)

(Tell them why you are reaching out)

(Thank them for reading)

(Insert your company, organization or brand)

THE TOOLS

New tools are continuously evolving to give marketers a unique opportunity to market more effectively. Rather than focusing on what tools are working right now, because they likely have already changed, I want to turn your attention to where to find them.

As I have said before, Google is your best friend. If you have questions about how to edit a video, set up a social media scheduling software, or how to make a GIF, Google has the answer for you.

PAY ATTENTION TO YOUR THRESHOLD

There will come a point when you will realize you can't do everything, and that's OK! It took me a while to understand—I was perfectly happy doing everything by myself. However, as I began to scale, I realized I just didn't have the time to do everything I wanted to do. I was actually stuck for months until I learned of the Pareto principle. The Pareto principle, or 80/ 20 rule, says that 20 percent of what you do accounts for 80 percent of the outcome you have. I decided to apply this principle to a problem I was having with scaling my content.

I love creating content, but I just didn't have enough time to create more content. I was spending more time editing the videos than making the videos. The 20 percent was accounting for 80 percent of my happiness in marketing.

I decided to try outsourcing some of the editing aspects I don't enjoy. The first video that I outsourced cost me $1 and had a turnaround time of eleven minutes. I liked the quality of the video; I decided to do an experiment for a week and test out how outsourcing this skill could help me.

For the last week, I have outsourced five more videos at an average cost of a $1 a minute to get captioned.

Though outsourcing seemed costly at the time, I realized that on average I was saving twelve minutes on each video I was getting captioned. This investment turned out to save time, which I would now use to create more content and in turn generate more meaningful relationships.

This chapter has no checklist, but I do want to emphasize that you have to allocate your time properly for your marketing efforts. There is no shortcut, cheat codes, or easy way around this. That being said, investing time and energy into your brand will yield massive dividends for much longer.

"The present time has one advantage over every other – it is our own."

—CHARLES CALEB COLTON

CHAPTER 20

SUCCESS LEAVES CLUES

"Where there is unity there is always victory."

—PUBLILIUS SYRUS

"No great marketing decisions have ever been made on qualitative data."

—JOHN SCULLEY

"THE TWO BRAINS"

As a marketer, you will continuously be implementing and refining your marketing efforts, but how will you know what is working and what is not?

You have to combine and learn to leverage the two brains.

You are often classified in life as a person who is either more left– or right-brained. If you're more analytical and methodical in your thinking, then you would be classified as being more *left-brained*. If you tend to be more creative or artistic, you're thought to be more *right-brained*.

As a child, I was more right-brained; I thrived off of being able to use my creativity and imagination to solve problems. Oddly, I decided I wanted to go to medical school.

I soon learned success in marketing requires you to employ both the creative and analytical brains. You have to balance being an artist and a scientist at the same time; it is in this balance where the magic happens.

I was completely unaware of this principle until I met Dennis Yu. Dennis is the cofounder and CEO of BlitzMetrics, a company that specializes in strategy and performance management of paid advertising for social media. Apart from being an author and a contributor to some of digital marketing's most notable publications, such as *Adweek* and Social Media Examiner, Dennis works closely with companies like Facebook and Google.

Dennis is an engineer by trade—a math guy, someone you wouldn't necessarily expect to be one of the top digital marketers in the world. However, with a record and twenty years of experience, he has definitely proven his abilities, yet he wasn't always this successful. As I mentioned earlier, you need both the creative and analytical sides of the brain to be successful. Dennis discovered this while working at American Airlines.

"I launched a couple of campaigns in the early 2000s to promote purchasing airline tickets online. Early on I struggled to increase this purchase rate [plane tickets sold] even with all the data I had. Not because I couldn't analyze it well, but because I was still looking at the problem from only an analytical standpoint."

He needed to learn the emotions behind why customers were not purchasing tickets online. He soon uncovered they had security concerns and were skeptical of whether they were getting the best deal or not. He investigated his customer's psychology and started to create plans that appealed to their emotions, as well as an incentive which would increase the transaction. He went to work, and through understanding the psychology, he was able to launch a program that educated the public about the enhanced security measures and offer a five thousand-mile booking bonus on top of a low-price guarantee.

"By understanding the customer's psychology and offering an incentive of guaranteed low price with 5000 miles I was able to blend those two brains, the creative and the analytical sides."

WE NEED BOTH

Dennis discovered the sweet spot, the perfect balance that leads to remarkable results. He approaches marketing in a way that breaks it down into measurements and optimizes results. Digital marketing enables us to sell at scale yet to do so one has to design a process that makes people interested in your product, service, or idea and moves to purchase it.

Digital marketing is a challenge—there is so much data and so many tools, it looks seems technology has all the power. The real power is in the actual strategies you develop. Technology is continuously evolving, and just because a tool or system works today, doesn't mean it will tomorrow. Thus, we have to learn to combine the analytical left brain and creative right brain because digital marketing is a mixed discipline.

How do you find harmony between these two traits?

Though it can be difficult at times, there are two fundamentals you have to consider: business metrics and storytelling.

"Business metrics are the cost per lead, claim, click, call, some metric that helps drive money to your company."

There is a business metric we are trying to optimize. If you don't know that, it doesn't matter how useful your tools are or how much training you have—without a clear goal, you will never know if your efforts are moving you closer to or further from it. Once you have those business metrics, you then break them down into diagnostic metrics.

"A diagnostic metric is usually a derived metric such as what is the click-through rate, or if you are looking at something like a cost of sale as a business metric, you will break it down into cost per click and conversation rate."

It's a secondary metric to help us troubleshoot if a business metric is not where it needs to be. For example, "if sales are down that is the business metric, but then what are the diagnostic metrics that will determine what is causing it. Is it because our marketing campaign is not good, is it because of seasonality or whatever else it could be around. More than likely it is because of number two, their storytelling."

People jump into the tools first, but they should first understand the importance of their ability to tell stories. We as marketers need to understand is that people, regardless of the platform, are still people who happen to be on the Internet.

Think about that—anyone who signs up for your list or goes to a landing page is still a real human, are they not? Real humans are using multiple channels both in the physical and digital world. It is so important to focus on building real relationships, regardless if they're online or off because relationships are formed on the same foundation, trust through storytelling.

"The basis of communication always boils down to the stories we tell, whether it be about an event we witnessed or a purchase we made."

The main thing that Dennis has seen work is storytelling, a perfect blend of both sides of one's brain. You can create emotion in using storytelling to make your content much more compelling—humans buy from humans, not companies. He has generated so much success by creating videos that are filmed to tell one story, not to generalize. A story is about a particular moment in time, and through condensing it down to a minute, you are forced to make the message clear and meaningful.

"These videos do exceptionally well because you create content that is short, concise and authentic, which intern builds trust and has a higher probability of turning into a sale organically."

And how do you know if it is successful? You look at the data generated from the story.

Digital marketing may seem like constant chaos. However, at its core, we can see that it only entails analytical story-telling. We can use stories to measure how well our digital marketing is working and how best to optimize it, merging the left and right brain.

CASE STUDY: TIM FERRISS

- In 2006, Timothy Ferriss and his publisher were searching for a title for his book about productivity, outsourcing, and mini-retirements. He took his six titles and decided to implement a test and let data determine which was best. He "developed a Google AdWords campaign for each. He bid on keywords related to the book's content including '401k' and 'language learning': when those keywords formed part of someone's search on Google, the prospective title popped up as a headline and the advertisement text would be the subtitle." He ran this campaign for about a week, and for under $200 he used data to determine the winner. He "admitted that the winners, *The 4-Hour Work Week: Escape 9-5, Live Any-where,* and *Join the New Rich,* were not his first choices. In hindsight, it's hard to imagine *Broadband* and *White Sand* generating the same buzz."[1]

The 4-Hour Work Week was a smashing success based on the data that was gathered, and it opened the gates for Tim Ferris. He now knew what his audience wanted and set out to create more content. Expert marketers don't rely on their own beliefs or assumptions to guide their decisions; they test everything. Tim would take the same principle into building a story around the book, which would ultimately lead to over a million copies of the book being sold. The story was there at the right point in time and the data provided what would be impactful.

MY STORY OF THE PRINCIPLE:

I used to struggle with this topic because I would just create content for the sake of creating content. I was essentially throwing darts in a dark room. Now, however, I focus on delivering the same topic in different manners and test out how it is received.

For example, I was exploring podcasting but didn't know what topic I wanted to speak about. I experimented with a podcast as I did with posts on my social platforms. I analyzed the engagement of my content over the span of a month. In that period, I tested out topics I thought would be compelling to talk about for the listener and that I liked talking about. I tested out marketing, entrepreneurship, mind-set, my journey, and a host of other topics. I discovered that the most engaging content was about marketing tips.

People enjoyed a minute podcast style post on marketing trends. Thus, I used data from different styles and messages to find out what my audiences wanted and what I wanted to deliver.

ACTION CHECKLIST

Each platform and medium on which you distribute content has its metrics, and I recommend doing a Google search to uncover these. The first step will be to find out what metrics matter and how to increase the ones that matter.

Start by Googling phrases such as:

- What are the metrics for **(enter the name of the platform)**?

- How do I increase **(specific metric)** for **(enter the name of the platform)**?

- What are the best ways to increase **(specific metric)** in **(enter the name of the platform)**?

- What are the best ways to increase **(specific metric)** in **(enter the name of the platform)** for **(enter your industry)**?

Regardless of platforms, these are the general analytics terms you should know:

- *Impressions*: These can be of text, audio, or video content. An impression means that the piece of content was seen by a person, but no action was necessarily taken.

- *View*: A view is similar to an impression, but this is usually only geared to videos. A video was watched for a minimum of three seconds; it does not mean direct action was necessarily taken.

- *Likes:* This indicator shows that a person took direct action. It is the least engaging action one can take, but it's engagement nonetheless and is an excellent indication of the platform's algorithm.

- *Comments:* A comment is one of the best examples of social engagement. A comment means your content appealed to your audience so much that it was awarded review, which can be positive or negative, from the user. This type of content will be deemed the best by the platform's algorithm.

- *Shares/retweets:* A share is one of the best indicators of content recognition. It indicates that the person is willing to share your content with their audience.

Don't lose focus on your goals and pay attention to what metrics get you closer to that goal.

"Stories are data with soul."

—BRENÉ BROWN

CONCLUSION

———

Why did you first decide to become a marketer? Was it a way to start a new career? Have more impact on the world? Or just understand how to get what you are selling to the right customers?

Regardless of the reason you did it, we did it. Because we're all marketers.

WHY DID THIS BOOK FOCUS ON TWENTY PRINCIPLES?

It's simple—we were never taught this. I never had a class that taught me about branding and marketing. Unless you get a degree in it, I bet you didn't, either.

I don't think there is one person to blame—I just know in my heart that being able to communicate and sell an idea is far too important not to know. This book focused on what you need to know to give you a strong foundation for successful marketing.

Marketing shouldn't just be left to people who get a degree in it; in the end, we market ourselves every day. That's why this book is so important. I wanted to create a guide that would break down what makes the top marketers so successful. Why? Because I couldn't find one.

When I decided to get serious about marketing, I had no idea where to start. Everywhere I looked, I couldn't find an easy way to learn the basics. Each time I picked up a book, watched a Ted talk, or listened to a podcast, I felt behind. There was no resource that explained marketing in an easy and effective way.

It was out of luck that I discovered the principles of marketing. These eighteen principles shaped my marketing career and serve as the springboard for becoming a successful marketer today, and that's what I want for you.

I know how confusing and disheartening it can be to get started in marketing—I was in your shoes not too long ago. I found it important to write about the principles of marketing purely because every profession is built on a foundation of principles, just like school.

You can't take a three hundred level class when you don't understand what happened in the one hundred or two hundred level classes. There is a natural progression of knowledge, and this book is your one hundred level class. It wouldn't be as meaningful to discuss the tactics, techniques, best practices, tips, fads, tools, and platforms, because they are always changing. Just look at all the social media sites such as Myspace or Vine that have come and gone.

THE PRINCIPLES

Each person highlighted in this book embodies a principle that has made them successful in marketing. They, too, started out knowing nothing, just like you and me. They, too, had to start with a strong foundation. They, too, had to learn about the principles.

The principles are so important that I wanted to summarize them all one last time.

Principle 1: The New Game

In "The New Game," we learned there is a new playing field of marketing. Shama Hyder walks us through the transition that occurred in the last several years, especially the transition to social media. It is so important to understand it because if you don't know the new rules of the game, how can you ever prosper?

Principle 2: Make It Spread

In "Make It Spread," we learned the importance of being remarkable from Seth Godin. You can have the best product or service in the world, but if no one knows about it, what's the point? This principle encourages you to market in order for your brands story to leave the screen and be spread throughout the world.

Principle 3: Branded

In "Branded," we learned that a company's brand isn't just a name or a logo—it's so much more. Michael Dubin takes as through the story of Dollar Shave Club and how a company that sells razors can go from nothing to selling for a billion dollars. Why? Not because he had the best razors in the world, but because of brand.

Principle 4: Authenticity

In "Authenticity," we learned that trust isn't a right—it's earned. How can you earn it? By being authentic in your content, business practices, the way you treat the people around you, and your marketing. Krista Fabrick breaks down for us how you and I can mark in an authentic way digitally and through social media.

Principle 5: Riches in Niches

"Riches in Niches" broke down the importance of having and carving out a niche for you. It isn't enough to try and market to everyone; that just won't work. You don't have the time, money, or influence to do that. Instead, Greg Head walked us through how we can discover our own niche and win within it.

Principle 6: Culture Role

In "Culture Role," we were asked a very important question: what is your role in culture? Steve Babcock showed us that for you to stand out, you have to define your role and pursue it. Legacy and reputation no longer cut it; your customers want to see you in the role you have crafted.

Principle 7: Attention

In "Attention," we learned from Gary Vaynerchuck about why your customers' attention is so important to find, understand, and serve as the basis for your content. We also learned that in this new world of marketing, some media and ways of marketing are underpriced, while some others are overpriced.

Principle 8: End It

"End It" focused on understanding what your end goal is, even before you create your marketing plan. Wendy Stevens told us that people care more about what you, your brand, service, or product can do for them. Does it get them closer to where they want to go? Are you telling the story that is right for them? Outcomes matter, so start with the outcome you want first.

Principle 9: Message It

Throughout "Message It," we learned that customers in the new game desire to know what message you and your brand have. Casey Neistat showed us that a simple, understandable, and relatable message has the power to spread your brand far and wide. Spend time on your message, craft it to fit your image, and then share it with the world.

Principle 10: Be Perennial

In "Be Perennial," we learned that some content is more contextual than others. An investment in evergreen content takes just as much time than one in trendy content, but evergreen content significant longer. Ryan Holiday helped us create this evergreen content that, if done correctly, will pay dividends far longer for you and your brand.

Principle 11: Tell Me a Story

In "Tell Me a Story," we learned that with so much content out there, a story has a way to give your brand an edge because, as humans, we communicate best though stories. From prehistoric man to modern day monk, we thrive off of storytelling. What's stopping you from telling your story? We walked with Jay Shetty as we learned about telling your story with the world.

Principle 12: Social Selling

The days of mass marketing and spamming are slowly moving aside for the new kid on the block, social selling. For this principle, Chelsea Pietz shares her expertise in the new rules of selling online, especially because of the massive opportunity that the Internet has given us. Remember people buy from people.

Principle 13: Lead with Value

This principle teaches us that good things happen to use when we lead each intention with value. Positioning you brand in this way will help lay the foundation for interactions that turn spectators into raving fans. The path of Quentin Allums and Nike walked you through how to do just that.

Principle 14: The Three Es

Wonder how you can keep your audience engaged and coming back for more? Rachel Pedersen broke down the three Es of content. By learning to engage, educate, and entertain you have a far better chance to build a meaningful relationship with your audience.

Principle 15: Content Series

Want to market like some of the biggest companies in the world? Vincent Orleck in "The Series" walked you through a strategy that is engaging and brings in your audience over a period of time through a content series. Content series are a way to bring in the three Es in a fun and unique way.

Principle 16: Experiment

The new game isn't stagnant—it is always changing and evolving. To stay on top of it, constantly experimenting with new mediums, content strategies, and ways to present your marketing is a priority. With Mark Metry's help, you learned how experimenting can truly alter your business.

Principle 17: Resourcefulness

In "Resourcefulness," we learned you will never know all the information or have all the resources or experiences you want, but that's OK. Justin Nguyen helped you see the resources you do have as exactly what you and your brand need to launch yourself to a whole new level.

Principle 18: Customer service

In "Customer Service," you learn that marketing isn't just about the content on your social media accounts, website, or brochures. The largest piece we don't focus on is our customer service. Jay Baer showed us why it's so important to respond to customers whether their engagement is positive or negative, because customer service matters tremendously in the new game.

Principle 19: Time

The one resource we all can't get enough of is time. As you know, where you spend your time is important, and we don't have the luxury to buy more of it. I walked you through a few ways to streamline your time in marketing to be more effective and impactful.

Principle 20: Success Leaves Clues

Success leaves clues, and it's our job to put those clues together in order to find meaning. Dennis Yu and Tim Ferriss both showed us that analytics matter. Each platform is different, so learn what metrics actually matter and use them to refine your marketing efforts in order to have massive effects.

THANK YOU

You have now made it to the end! Does it feel good? I sure hope so! Just remember, I want this book to be your guide and serve as a stepping stone to marketing. As you get further into marketing, continue to use this book as a tool. Skip around, use the checklists, and apply the lessons until it becomes second nature to you.

Once again, welcome to the club, marketer!

ACKNOWLEDGEMENTS

———

First and foremost, I would like to thank my family. Mom and Dad, thank you for all of your love and support. Mom, thank you for always pushing me to find the good and the joy of life. Dad, thank you for being there for me, always encouraging me to be my best, push a little more, and reach for the stars.

Thank you to my mentors. Sasha, for giving me the guidance, love, wisdom, and friendship that has enabled me to become the marketer I am today. Tudor, thank you for always encouraging me to strive for continuous growth with so much kindness and empathy. Paul, thank you for opening my eyes to the world of business and showing me that regardless of age, you can make a difference.

Thank you to my friends. Larissa for being there for me day in and day out, your feedback made a world of difference to the book. Max, for pushing me to find new ways to connect with my audience and providing so many insights. Alison and Krista, for helping to find my voice, guiding me and help me put out my very first video on the internet.

A HUGE thank you to the team at New Degree Press, Eric, Brian, Carson, Zoran, Leila, Ryan and Katherine for supporting me along this book creation journey. Special thank you to Eric and Brian Bies for working with me to create this book and helping me to find my passion.

While creating this book, I had the unique opportunity to interview many fascinating people within the marketing industry. Each conversation taught me something new, something foundational, and was a chance, and each conversation brought me closer to making this cook a reality.

I want to thank those who I have interviewed for the book; your insights and wisdom made this book possible. I want to take a moment to thank everyone who I interviewed individually:

Krista Fabrick (Marketing Consultant, Speaker & Professor)

Greg Head (CEO of Scaling Point)

Steve Babcock (CCO+ Creator / Speaker / Founder)

Wendy Stevens (Guerrilla Marketing Consultant)

Chelsea Pietz (Social Media Coach, National Director of Social Sales)

Vincent Orleck (Social Media Manager, ASU Knowledge Enterprise)

Mark Metry (Host of Top 100 Humans 2.0 Podcast & Speaker)

Justin Nguyen (CEO and co-founder Of The GetChoGrindUp Movement)

Dennis Yu (CEO of BlitzMetrics)

I'd like to also thank everyone who pre-ordered my book. Your financial support made this book and it's publication possible. I'd like to take a moment to individually thank everyone who pre-ordered my book:

Tudor Melville   Eric Koester
Al Bergeron   Paul Brunoforte
Jani Tuomi   Zhara Davies
Bogdan Padua   Moustafa Madkaur
Edwin Radtke   Gary J. Lanham

Benjamin Morazan

Nima Sadeghi

Jason Fox

Adam Posner

Evalina Burger

Patti Milligan

Jordan Paris

Sydney Pisano

Max Bartolomea

Sasha Rowe

Lynne LaMaster

Shaleni Henriquez

Michael E Navarro

Estela Barraza

Justin Ito-Adler

Daniella Banda

Sean McKenna s

Jeremiah Stillings j

Isaac Jeong

William E Preble

Ty Banks

Aaron Watson

Sterling Loucks

Nicole Ramirez

Kimberley Richardson

David Barnes

Siddharth Das

Dr. Rick Hall

Thank you to everyone. Your financial support allowed me to transform countless pages of notes and interviews into the the book you have read.

APPENDIX

INTRODUCTION

1. Maryville Online. (2019). *11 Modern Marketing Skills for Business Innovators to Master.* [online] Available at: https://online.maryville.edu/blog/11-modern-marketing-skills-for-business-innovators-to-master/ [Accessed 9 Jun. 2019].

2. Digital Marketing Blueprint. (2019). *What is Content Promotion and How it works? | Digital Marketing Blueprint.* [online] Available at: https://www.digitalmarketingblueprint.org/blog/content-promotion/ [Accessed 9 Jun. 2019].

3. Kafka, P. and Molla, R. (2019). *2017 was the year digital ad spending finally beat TV.* [online] Vox. Available at: https://www.vox.com/2017/12/4/16733460/2017-digital-ad-spend-advertising-beat-tv [Accessed 9 Jun. 2019].

CHAPTER 1

1. YouTube. (2019). *2017 Gwyn David Lecture presented by Shama Hyder.* [online] Available at: https://www.youtube.com/watch?v=hDPFKUXP6NA [Accessed 9 Jun. 2019].

2. YouTube. (2019). *How To Become A Social Media Zen Master [Interview With Shama Hyder]*. [online] Available at: https://www.youtube.com/watch?v=nNxt-f42obzI [Accessed 9 Jun. 2019].

3. YouTube. (2019). *2017 Gwyn David Lecture presented by Shama Hyder*.

4. YouTube. (2019). *2017 Gwyn David Lecture presented by Shama Hyder*.

5. Prnewswire.com. (2019). *Influencer Marketing Update: Non-Celebrity Influencers 10 Times More Likely to Drive In-Store Purchases*. [online] Available at: https://www.prnewswire.com/news-releases/influencer-marketing-update-non-celebrity-influencers-10-times-more-likely-to-drive-in-store-purchases-300241060.html [Accessed 9 Jun. 2019].

6. Ahmed, M. (2019). *Is Social Media the Biggest Influencer of Buying Decisions?*. [online] Social Media Today. Available at: https://www.socialmediatoday.com/marketing/masroor/2015-05-28/social-media-biggest-influencer-buying-decisions [Accessed 9 Jun. 2019].

CHAPTER 2

1. Godin, S. (2019). *Transcript of "How to get your ideas to spread"*. [online] Ted.com. Available at: https://www.ted.com/talks/seth_godin_on_sliced_bread/transcript?language=en [Accessed 9 Jun. 2019].

2. Jiwa, B. (2019). *The secret to spreading ideas: Bernadette Jiwa at TEDxPerth*. [online] YouTube. Available at: https://www.youtube.com/watch?v=orRJtNK-Cz_U [Accessed 9 Jun. 2019].

CHAPTER 3

1. Dubin, M. (2019). *How Michael Dubin Built a Brand Identity Out of a Commodity*. [online] Inc.com. Available at: https://www.inc.com/video/how-michael-dubin-built-a-brand-identity-out-of-a-commodity.html [Accessed 9 Jun. 2019].

2. Trop, J. (2019). *How Dollar Shave Club's Founder Built a $1 Billion Company That Changed the Industry*. [online] Entrepreneur. Available at: https://www.entrepreneur.com/article/290539 [Accessed 9 Jun. 2019].

3. YouTube. (2019). *DollarShaveClub.com - Our Blades Are F***ing Great.* [online] Available at: https://www.youtube.com/watch?v=ZUG9qYTJMsI [Accessed 9 Jun. 2019].

4. REIM, G. (2019). *Dollar Shave Club's CEO Michael Dubin explains his approach to branding & viral videos.* [online] Built In Los Angeles. Available at: https://www.builtinla.com/2014/09/03/dollar-shave-clubs-ceo-michael-dubin-explains-his-approach-branding-viral-videos [Accessed 9 Jun. 2019].

5. Geller, M. and Shakil, I. (2019). *Unilever sharpens P&G rivalry by buying Dollar Shave Club.* [online] U.K. Available at: https://uk.reuters.com/article/uk-dollar-shave-m-a-unilvr-idUKKCN100075 [Accessed 9 Jun. 2019].

6. Geller, M. and Shakil, I. (2019). *Unilever sharpens P&G rivalry by buying Dollar Shave Club.*

7. Geller, M. and Shakil, I. (2019). *Unilever sharpens P&G rivalry by buying Dollar Shave Club.*

Cdn2.hubspot.net. (2019). *Finding Your Brand Differentiator.* [online] Available at: https://cdn2.hubspot.net/hubfs/309297/Premium_Content/ERVH_0348_FindYourDifferentiator_eBook_0112.pdf [Accessed 9 Jun. 2019].

Dubin, M. (2019). *Secrets from a Genius Marketer | Mike Dubin, CEO of Dollar Shave Club.* [online] YouTube. Available at: https://www.youtube.com/watch?v=HIbIlbGbdCQ [Accessed 9 Jun. 2019].

CHAPTER 4

1. Cassidy, P. (2019). *Survey Finds Consumers Crave Authenticity - and User-Generated Content Delivers.* [online] Social Media Today. Available at: https://www.socialmediatoday.com/news/survey-finds-consumers-crave-authenticity-and-user-generated-content-deli/511360/ [Accessed 9 Jun. 2019].

2. The Economist. (2019). *It's the real thing.* [online] Available at: https://www.economist.com/business/2015/11/14/its-the-real-thing [Accessed 9 Jun. 2019].

3. Digital Wellbeing. (2019). *'Brand Authenticity' Definition and Measurement Scale [Study].* [online] Available at: https://digitalintelligencetoday.com/new-brand-authenticity-scale-released-how-authentic-are-you/ [Accessed 9 Jun. 2019].

CHAPTER 5

1. Alexa Blog. (2019). *Niche Marketing: Definition, Examples, and 4 Steps to Develop a Strategy - Alexa Blog.* [online] Available at: https://blog.alexa.com/niche-marketing/ [Accessed 9 Jun. 2019].

2. Revolvy.com. (2019). *"Untuckit" on Revolvy.com.* [online] Available at: https://www.revolvy.com/page/Untuckit [Accessed 9 Jun. 2019].

CHAPTER 6

1. Definitions.net. (2019). *What does brands mean?.* [online] Available at: https://www.definitions.net/definition/brands [Accessed 9 Jun. 2019].

2. Klara, R. (2019). *From Ridgemont High to 'Damn, Daniel,' Vans Is Still Kicking It at 50.* [online] Adweek.com. Available at: https://www.adweek.com/brand-marketing/ridgemont-high-damn-daniel-vans-still-kicking-it-50-170130/ [Accessed 9 Jun. 2019].

CHAPTER 7

1. YouTube. (2019). *How to Take Advantage of Opportunities in Business | Auckland, NZ Keynote 2018.* [online] Available at: https://www.youtube.com/watch?v=sr2fSEgSGZY [Accessed 9 Jun. 2019].

2. Vaynerchuk, G. (2019). *When Will Marketers Talk About Attention, Not Impressions?.* [online] GaryVaynerchuk.com. Available at: https://www.garyvaynerchuk.com/when-will-marketers-talk-about-attention-not-impressions/ [Accessed 9 Jun. 2019].

3. GaryVaynerchuk.com. (2019). *Number One Waste of Time? Trying to Convert Your Customer.* [online] Available at: https://www.garyvaynerchuk.com/number-one-waste-of-time-trying-to-convert-your-customer/ [Accessed 9 Jun. 2019].

4. Vaynerchuk, G. (2019). *Digital Marketing Agency | Sasha Group.* [online] GaryVaynerchuk.com. Available at: https://www.garyvaynerchuk.com/digital-marketing-agency/ [Accessed 9 Jun. 2019].

5. Vaynerchuk, G. (2019). *Stop Complaining! Put in the time!.* [online] GaryVaynerchuk.com. Available at: https://www.garyvaynerchuk.com/stop-complaining-put-in-the-time/ [Accessed 9 Jun. 2019].

6. https://threesixtyeight.com. (2019). *Crushing It: 10 Lessons from Gary Vaynerchuk*. [online] Available at: https://threesixtyeight.com/insights/crushingit/ [Accessed 9 Jun. 2019].

7.Teixeira, T. (2019). *The Rising Cost of Consumer Attention: Why You Should Care, and What You Can Do about It*. [online] Hbs.edu. Available at: http://www.hbs.edu/faculty/Publication%20Files/14-055_2ef21e7e-7529-4864-b0f0-c64e4169e17f.pdf [Accessed 9 Jun. 2019].

8.Teixeira, T. (2019). *The Rising Cost of Consumer Attention: Why You Should Care, and What You Can Do about It*.

CHAPTER 8

1. Wendy Stevens. (2019). *Biography of Wendy Stevens - Wendy Stevens*. [online] Available at: https://coachwendystevens.com/biography-of-wendy-stevens/ [Accessed 9 Jun. 2019].[1]

2. Lamotte, C. (2019). *Summary of 4-Hour Workweek - Tim Ferriss*. [online] Real Marketing Specialists. Available at: https://www.real-m.com/a-summary-of-the-4-hour-workweek-tim-ferriss/ [Accessed 9 Jun. 2019].

CHAPTER 9

1. YouTube. (2019). *iPod's Dirty Secret - from 2003*. [online] Available at: https://www.youtube.com/watch?v=SuTcavAz0pg [Accessed 9 Jun. 2019].

2. Frankel, D. (2019). *HBO nabs the Neistats*. [online] Variety. Available at: https://variety.com/2009/scene/markets-festivals/hbo-nabs-the-neistats-1118001386/ [Accessed 9 Jun. 2019].

3. Steele, B. (2019). *Casey Neistat, Three Things I've Learned From The Man Behind the Camera*. [online] Benjamin Steele. Available at: https://www.benjaminsteele.us/blog/2016/09/21/casey-neistat-three-things-ive-learned-from-the-man-behind-the-camera [Accessed 9 Jun. 2019].

4. Frankel, D. (2019). *HBO nabs the Neistats*. [online] Variety. Available at: https://variety.com/2009/scene/markets-festivals/hbo-nabs-the-neistats-1118001386/ [Accessed 9 Jun. 2019].

5. YouTube. (2019). *Bike Lanes by Casey Neistat*. [online] Available at: https://www.youtube.com/watch?v=bzE-IMaegzQ [Accessed 9 Jun. 2019].

6. Kunes, A. (2019). *Announcement: Casey Neistat is Speaking at Hustle Con*. [online] Hustle Con. Available at: https://hustlecon.com/how-casey-neistat-used-youtube-to-sell-his-startup-to-cnn/ [Accessed 9 Jun. 2019].

7. Axelrod, G. (2019). *How to Be Heard: Casey Neistat on Marketing's New Normal – Drift*. [online] Drift. Available at: https://www.drift.com/blog/casey-neistat-how-to-be-heard/ [Accessed 9 Jun. 2019].

8. YouTube. (2019). *Make It Count*. [online] Available at: https://www.youtube.com/watch?v=WxfZkMm3wcg [Accessed 9 Jun. 2019].

CHAPTER 10

1. Merriam-webster.com. (2019). *Definition of EVERGREEN*. [online] Available at: https://www.merriam-webster.com/dictionary/evergreen [Accessed 9 Jun. 2019].

2. YouTube. (2019). *RYAN HOLIDAY, PERENNIAL SELLER, MOMENTO MORI & SELLING WHAT YOU BELIEVE IN | #ASKGARYVEE 262*. [online] Available at: https://www.youtube.com/watch?v=QTbQMbRDZj4 [Accessed 9 Jun. 2019].

3. YouTube. (2019). *Laracon 2018 - Perennial Seller - Ryan Holiday*. [online] Available at: https://www.youtube.com/watch?v=kKGkURY-QsA [Accessed 9 Jun. 2019].

4. YouTube. (2019). *Laracon 2018 - Perennial Seller - Ryan Holiday*.

5. YouTube. (2019). *Perennial Seller: The Art of MAKING and MARKETING Work that LASTS ft. @ryanholiday*. [online] Available at: https://www.youtube.com/watch?v=KSuzlOoWo-Q [Accessed 9 Jun. 2019].

6. YouTube. (2019). *Ryan Holiday, Director of Marketing, American Apparel*. [online] Available at: https://www.youtube.com/watch?v=GKoMgCvlr1U [Accessed 9 Jun. 2019].

7. YouTube. (2019). *Laracon 2018 - Perennial Seller - Ryan Holiday*.

8. An, M. (2019). *Compounding Blog Posts: What They Are and Why They Matter*. [online] Blog.hubspot.com. Available at: https://blog.hubspot.com/news-trends/compounding-blog-posts-what-they-are-and-why-they-matter [Accessed 9 Jun. 2019].

CHAPTER 11

1. Jay Shetty. (2019). *My Story - Jay Shetty*. [online] Available at: https://jayshetty.me/my-story/ [Accessed 9 Jun. 2019].

2. Lewis Howes. (2019). *Cultivate the Modern Day Mind of a Monk with Jay Shetty*. [online] Available at: https://lewishowes.com/podcast/cultivate-a-monk-mindset-jay-shetty/ [Accessed 9 Jun. 2019].

3. Zak, P. (2019). *Why Your Brain Loves Good Storytelling*. [online] Harvard Business Review. Available at: https://hbr.org/2014/10/why-your-brain-loves-good-storytelling [Accessed 9 Jun. 2019].

4. Zak, P. (2019). *Why Your Brain Loves Good Storytelling*.

CHAPTER 12

1. Peitz, C. (2019). *WATCH: Why life in front of the camera is best for your biz*. [online] Inman. Available at: https://www.inman.com/2018/07/27/watch-chelsea-peitz-on-why-life-in-front-of-the-camera-is-best-for-business/ [Accessed 9 Jun. 2019].

CHAPTER 13

1. YouTube. (2019). *#36 Quentin Allums | Epic Journey of Becoming a LinkedIn Community Storyteller*. [online] Available at: https://www.youtube.com/watch?v=DXrv9G7H_yU [Accessed 9 Jun. 2019].

2. Rose, R. (2019). *Want to Prove Content's Success? Stop Measuring It*. [online] Content Marketing Institute. Available at: https://contentmarketinginstitute.com/2018/08/stop-measuring-content/ [Accessed 9 Jun. 2019].

CHAPTER 14

1. Pedersen, R. (2019). *Rachel Pedersen: Social Media Tactics to Go Viral World-Wide | EOFire*. [online] Entrepreneurs on Fire with John Lee Dumas. Available at: https://www.eofire.com/podcast/rachelpedersen/ [Accessed 9 Jun. 2019].

2. Pedersen, R. (2019). *How to Grow Your Facebook Following Organically*. [online] Facebook Watch. Available at: https://www.facebook.com/watch/?v=1829449887165684 [Accessed 9 Jun. 2019].

CHAPTER 16

1. Metry, M. (2019). *36 Questions that Fundamentally Changed the Course of My Life.* [online] Linkedin.com. Available at: https://www.linkedin.com/pulse/36-questions-fundamentally-changed-course-my-life-mark-metry/ [Accessed 9 Jun. 2019].

2. Larson, K. (2019). *Cosmetic brand L'Oréal succeeds in the digital age - Think with Google.* [online] Think with Google. Available at: https://www.thinkwithgoogle.com/marketing-resources/data-measurement/lor%C3%A9al-cosmetics-beauty-brand-experimentation/ [Accessed 9 Jun. 2019].

CHAPTER 17

1. Nguyen, J. (2019). *Hedging Better |.* [online] YouTube. Available at: https://www.youtube.com/watch?v=VxiqCRqE-4A [Accessed 9 Jun. 2019].

2. Into The Gloss. (2019). *Sophia Amoruso, Founder & CEO, Nasty Gal.* [online] Available at: http://intothegloss.com/2012/09/sophia-amoruso-founder-ceo-nasty-gal/ [Accessed 9 Jun. 2019].

CHAPTER 18

1. Baer, J. (2019).

#CMWorld 2016 - How to Use Customer Service to Create Killer Content - Jay Baer. [online] YouTube. Available at: https://www.youtube.com/watch?v=2t4x-ZudSlug [Accessed 9 Jun. 2019].

2. Gingiss, D. (2019). *Focus on Customer Service: Southwest Airlines.* [online] Social Media Today. Available at: https://www.socialmediatoday.com/special-columns/focus-customer-service-southwest-airlines [Accessed 9 Jun. 2019].

3. Ipfs.io. (2019). *Jay Baer.* [online] Available at: https://ipfs.io/ipfs/QmXoypizjW3WknFiJnKLwHCnL72vedxjQkDDP1mXWo6uco/wiki/Jay_Baer.html [Accessed 9 Jun. 2019].

CHAPTER 20

1. Furr, R. (2019). *How to Test Book or Product Titles Using Google AdWords - Breakthrough Marketing Secrets.* [online] Breakthrough Marketing Secrets. Available at: https://www.breakthroughmarketingsecrets.com/blog/how-to-test-book-or-product-titles-using-google-adwords/ [Accessed 9 Jun. 2019].

Made in the USA
Monee, IL
26 October 2020

46147213R00157